Nordic Bakery
Cookbook

Nordic Bakery
Cookbook

Miisa Mink

Food photography by Peter Cassidy

Reportage photography by Marianna Wahlsten

RYLAND PETERS & SMALL
LONDON • NEW YORK

Finnish-born **Jali Wahlsten** had a vision of bringing Nordic 'dark rye bread, cinnamon buns and coffee' to London and in 2007 opened the Nordic Bakery in Soho. This, the bakery's first cookbook, was conceived by Jali's wife **Marianna Wahlsten**, a journalist and photographer, and written by **Miisa Mink**, an investor in the business. Marianna has written articles for Finnish and British publications, specializing in architecture, interiors and travel. Miisa comes from a family of passionate bakers. She has had a successful career in branding and design, but left the corporate life in 2007 to become a partner in the Nordic Bakery. The Nordic Bakery can be found in London's Soho, Marylebone and Baker Street. **www.nordicbakery.com**

Peter Cassidy is one of Europe's most talented photographers. He specializes in food and travel and his work frequently appears in magazines, including *Olive*, *delicious*, *She* and *Country Living*. For Ryland Peters & Small, he has previously photographed *Real Mexican Food*, *All You Knead is Bread*, *Flavours of Morocco* and the number one best-selling *The Hummingbird Bakery Cookbook*.

Food photography Peter Cassidy
Reportage photography and book concept
Marianna Wahlsten

Design and Photographic Art Direction
Steve Painter
Senior Editor Céline Hughes
Production Controller Toby Marshall
Art Director Leslie Harrington

Food Stylist Lizzie Harris
Prop Stylist Róisín Neild
Indexer Hilary Bird

Originally published in 2011.
This edition published in 2013
by Ryland Peters & Small
20–21 Jockey's Fields
London WC1R 4BW
and
519 Broadway, 5th Floor
New York, NY 10012

www.rylandpeters.com

10 9 8 7 6 5 4 3 2 1

Text © Miisa Mink 2011, 2013
Design and photographs
© Ryland Peters & Small 2011, 2013

Printed in China

ISBN: 978 1 84975 458 3

A CIP record for this book is available from the British Library.

The original edition is cataloged as follows:
Library of Congress Cataloging-in-Publication Data

Mink, Miisa.
 Nordic bakery cookbook / Miisa Mink ; food photography by Peter Cassidy ; reportage photography by Marianna Wahlsten.
  p. cm.
 Includes index.
 ISBN 978-1-84975-096-7
1. Baking--Finland. 2. Cooking, Scandinavian. 3. Cookbooks. I. Title.
 TX763.M54 2011
 641.5948--dc22

                    2010049694

Notes
• All spoon measurements are level, unless otherwise specified.
• All eggs are medium (UK) and large (US), unless otherwise specified, and should be used at room temperature. It is generally recommended that free-range eggs be used. Uncooked or partially cooked eggs should not be served to the very young, the very old, those with compromised immune systems, or to pregnant women.
• Ovens should be preheated to the specified temperature. Recipes in this book were tested using a regular oven. If using a fan oven, follow the manufacturer's instructions for adjusting temperatures.

Contents

Welcome to the Nordic Bakery

I grew up in Finland. My family spent every summer near Lake Saimaa, in the southeast of Finland, in an old farmhouse where my father was born. Throughout the summer, my parents dragged me through the forest picking mushrooms, blueberries and lingonberries. My father took me with him on fishing trips, so that by the age of 11 – before I even knew what a hamburger was – I knew how to scale a fish.

Knowing where food comes from and how to handle fresh ingredients is at the heart of the Nordic way of cooking. Whenever possible, we try to use ingredients direct from nature, either just caught or freshly picked. A typical Nordic meal might include a starter of wild mushroom soup with some rye bread or flatbread, followed by fresh fish served with seasonal greens and potatoes and some more bread. Buns, cakes or tarts are served for dessert with coffee after the meal. We use a lot of rye, oats and barley in our bread, and exotic spices like cardamom and cloves in our bakes.

Baking is a social activity. I remember my grandmother making a vanilla cake decorated with plenty of strawberries for my birthday every year. And at Christmas, the whole family had fun creating gingerbread men and star pastries together. Whenever I bake, a crowd gathers in my kitchen, drawn to the smell of fresh bread.

For me, baking and good food have always been about so much more than just filling stomachs. Nordic food is uncomplicated and honest. It is about appreciating the simple things in life, and bringing generations together to create memories.

Since design and branding are my profession, I have been able to combine my passion for pure, natural food and beautiful design at the Nordic Bakery. We have tried to provide a space where people can enjoy a cup of coffee and a cinnamon bun in a peaceful and uncluttered environment. The honesty of the food plays a very important part in this.

I hope this book conveys some of our principles and beliefs. Most of the recipes are very simple and easy to make; some require more time and effort, but are wonderful as weekend projects to linger over.

Enjoy!

Miisa Mink

Breads

Rye bread

Rye bread is the most traditional bread in Finland. In some parts of the country, it used to be the *only* bread that people baked. And in some areas, it was only baked a couple of times a year, then dried and enjoyed all year long. There are probably as many variations on rye bread as there are bakers, so we're sharing our own version here, which is very simple to make.

14 g/2 envelopes
(4½ teaspoons) easy-blend/
active dried yeast

900 ml–1 litre/4–4½ cups
lukewarm water

800 g/6 cups wholemeal/
dark rye flour

2 teaspoons sea salt

3 baking sheets, lined with baking parchment

Makes 3 loaves

Put the yeast in a large mixing bowl with 200 ml/1 cup of the lukewarm water and a couple of tablespoons of the flour. Stir well to mix. Cover with a clean dish towel and leave in a warm place overnight.

The next day, mix in the salt and remaining flour with enough lukewarm water to make a soft dough. Knead the dough on a lightly floured surface for a few minutes – it may be soft and sticky. Cover with the dish towel again and let prove in a warm place for 1–1½ hours, until doubled in size.

Punch down the dough, divide into three and roll into balls on the floured surface. Flatten each one into a disc and make a hole in the middle to form a ring. Transfer to the prepared baking sheets. Cover with the dish towel again and let rest in a warm place for 1 hour.

Preheat the oven to 220°C (425°F) Gas 7.

Dust the bread with flour and bake in the preheated oven for 30 minutes, or until nicely browned.

Open sandwich with gravad lax

Gravad lax

a whole salmon fillet, about 600 g/1¼ lbs., skin on

2 tablespoons coarse sea salt

1 teaspoon (caster) sugar

a handful of fresh dill, torn into small sprigs

2 tablespoons Cognac (optional)

Place the fillet on a large sheet of greaseproof paper, skin-side down. Sprinkle the salt and sugar evenly over the surface. Scatter the dill on top. Drizzle over the Cognac, if using.

Wrap the paper very tightly around the salmon. Take another sheet of greaseproof paper and wrap that tightly around the salmon too. Place on a dish, skin-side down, and refrigerate for 24 hours. Turn over after 12 hours.

For two open sandwiches

1 tablespoon mayonnaise

1 slice of Rye Bread (page 11), sliced in half

50 g/2 oz. gravad lax, thinly sliced

4 very thin slices of cucumber

a small handful of fresh dill, roughly chopped

Spread the mayonnaise on both pieces of bread. Top with the slices of salmon and cucumber and the dill.

We love gravad lax and we tend to serve it on many occasions and in many different ways. Why? Because it is very easy to make, it keeps for a couple of days and is so healthy and delicious. The recipe opposite makes a lot, but it is practical to use a whole fillet. Even better would be to buy an entire salmon and ask the fishmonger to fillet it for you. Then you can make the recipe as described opposite, but place the fillets on top of each other, skin-side out.

We have two recipes on how to use gravad lax in this book. First, it makes a great topping for an open sandwich (see opposite); you can use rye bread, rye baguette or archipelago bread. Secondly, there is a recipe for Salmon Coulibiac on page 44. If you have any leftovers, you can simply serve them as a starter/appetizer, thinly sliced with a little green salad, boiled new potatoes and rye bread on the side.

Rye baguettes

We make these individual baguettes for summer picnics and they are always a hit. They go well with soft cheese, such as Brie, and if you can get your hands on a jar of lingonberry jam, spoon some of that on top of the Brie.

250 ml/1 cup lukewarm water

7 g/1 envelope (2¼ teaspoons) easy-blend/active dried yeast

1 teaspoon sea salt

300 g/2⅓ cups strong white bread flour

100 g/¾ cup wholemeal/ dark rye flour

1 tablespoon rapeseed/ canola oil (or vegetable oil)

2 tablespoons golden syrup or pure maple syrup

50 g/½ cup raisins, chopped

2 baking sheets, lined with baking parchment

Makes 8 small baguettes

Put the water in a large mixing bowl with the yeast and whisk until it has dissolved. Add the salt and flours and mix quickly into a soft dough. Knead well on a lightly floured surface for a couple of minutes. Return to the bowl and add the remaining ingredients. Knead for a couple of minutes again. You should now have a firm dough. Sprinkle with flour, cover with a clean dish towel and let prove in a warm place for 1 hour, or until the dough has doubled in size.

Punch down the dough and divide it into eight on the lightly floured surface. Roll each portion into baguettes, about 4 cm/1¾ inches wide in the middle and slightly pointed at the ends. Arrange on the prepared baking sheets. Cover with the dish towel again and let prove in a warm place for 1 hour, or until the baguettes have doubled in size.

Preheat the oven to 240°C (475°F) Gas 9.

Dip a sharp knife in cold water and use to make 3 diagonal cuts on top of each baguette. Bake in the preheated oven for 10–12 minutes, or until golden brown.

Archipelago bread

The islands situated in the Archipelago Sea, part of the Baltic Sea, are famous for their traditional dark bread distinguished by the use of buttermilk and syrup among the ingredients. This bread polarizes opinion. Some people love it and some can't stand it because it is quite sweet. We belong to the absolute fans! The original recipe is made with buttermilk and hops, but we have simplified it. We encourage you to make this, as it's dead easy, tastes amazing, you will impress all your dinner guests and it keeps for several days. It goes very well with salmon, so try it with the gravad lax on page 12, or top it with Brussels pâté and pickles – these are two of our topping favourites.

500 ml/2¼ cups lukewarm milk

7 g/1 envelope (2¼ teaspoons) easy-blend/active dried yeast

100 ml/6½ tablespoons natural/plain yogurt

150 ml/⅔ cup golden syrup or pure maple syrup

150 g/1 generous cup barley flour

150 g/1 generous cup rolled (porridge) oats

250 g/2 cups wholemeal/ dark rye flour

250 g/2 cups strong wholemeal/whole-wheat bread flour

1 teaspoon sea salt

Glaze

1 tablespoon golden syrup or pure maple syrup

3 tablespoons hot water

2 non-stick 900-g/2-lb. loaf pans

Makes 2 loaves

Put the milk in a large mixing bowl with the yeast and whisk until it has dissolved. Add the yogurt and whisk to combine. Fold in the rest of the ingredients. There is no need to knead the dough; just mix it well to create a soft and sticky mixture.

Divide the mixture between the loaf pans, filling the pans only half full, as the dough will rise. Dip a spoon in water and use the back of it to press the mixture slightly down into the pans. Cover with a clean dish towel and let prove in a warm place for 2 hours.

Preheat the oven 170°C (325°F) Gas 3.

Bake the loaves in the preheated oven for 1 hour.

Meanwhile, make the glaze by putting the syrup and hot water in a small bowl and stirring until blended.

After 1 hour of the baking time, remove the loaves from the oven, brush some of the glaze over the tops and return to the oven for another 45 minutes, or until dark brown.

Remove the loaves from the oven and tip out of the pans onto a wire rack. Brush a little more glaze over them and let cool under the dish towel for 1 hour. Eat warm or cold. The bread will keep in an airtight container for several days.

Open sandwiches with herring salad

This is a classic sandwich at the Bakery, because herring is such a typical Nordic ingredient. Many people are afraid of the strong taste of herring, but this is the kind of recipe you need to get you accustomed to the taste, as we mix it with new potatoes and mayonnaise. Try these sandwiches for Sunday brunch.

150 g/5 oz. new potatoes

150 g/5 oz. mustard herring, diced

5 tablespoons mayonnaise

a small handful of fresh dill, finely chopped

6 slices of Archipelago Bread (page 16)

Makes 6

Boil the potatoes until cooked through, then drain and let cool. Peel off the skin and dice the flesh.

Mix the chopped potatoes, herring, mayonnaise and dill together in a small bowl. There is no need to season, as the herring is already full of flavour. Spread the mixture on top of the slices of bread.

Open sandwiches with summer salad

A very popular lunch option during the summer months at the Bakery, this suits those who don't get on with herring!

200 g/6 oz. new potatoes

¼ small onion, diced

⅓ cucumber, diced

2 tablespoons white wine vinegar

150 ml/⅔ cup sour cream

3 halves of Rye Baguette (page 15)

sea salt and freshly ground black pepper

Makes 3

Boil the potatoes until cooked through, then drain and let cool. Peel off the skin and dice the flesh.

Mix the chopped potatoes, onion and cucumber together in a small bowl. Put the vinegar and sour cream in a separate bowl and stir to combine. Add salt and black pepper to taste, then stir into the chopped potato mixture.

Spread the mixture on top of the baguette halves.

Carrot and oat rolls

For some reason it always creates a stir if we're back home in Finland and we hear that someone is baking bread rolls. These are our favourites and they are great, buttered, for breakfast or as a snack with ham or cheese.

300 ml/1¼ cups lukewarm water

7 g/1 envelope (2¼ teaspoons) easy-blend/active dried yeast

½–1 teaspoon sea salt

450 g/3½ cups strong white bread flour

50 g/½ cup rolled (porridge) oats

1 tablespoon rapeseed/canola oil (or vegetable oil)

2 medium carrots, finely grated

2 baking sheets, lined with baking parchment

Makes 12

Put the water in a large mixing bowl with the yeast and stir until it has dissolved. Add the salt and 300 g/2¼ cups of the flour and mix quickly into a dough. Knead well on a lightly floured surface for a couple of minutes. Add the oats and oil and knead again. Finally, add the grated carrots and the rest of the flour and knead for a couple of minutes again. You should now have a soft dough. It may also be a little sticky. Sprinkle with flour, cover with a clean dish towel and let prove in a warm place for 1 hour, or until doubled in size.

Punch down the dough and divide into four on a lightly floured surface. Divide each portion into three and roll into balls, then flatten just slightly. Dust all over with flour and arrange on the prepared baking sheets. Cover with the dish towel again and let prove in a warm place for 30 minutes. Preheat the oven to 200°C (400°F) Gas 6.

Bake the rolls in the preheated oven for 15 minutes, or until risen and golden.

LEFT Carrot and Oat Rolls

Potato rye bread

You need to start this a day in advance, but it is worth the effort. Eat it with soup or on its own. It's best eaten the day after baking.

500 g/1 lb. floury potatoes (e.g. King Edward), peeled and cut into small chunks

100 g/¾ cup rye flakes

300 g/2¼ cups wholemeal rye flour

25 g/1½ cakes fresh yeast or 7 g/1 envelope (2¼ teaspoons) easy-blend/active dried yeast

500 g/3⅔ cups strong white bread flour

100 ml/scant ½ cup golden syrup or pure maple syrup

½ tablespoon sea salt

½ tablespoon cumin seeds, freshly ground

2 baking sheets, lined with baking parchment

Makes 2 large loaves

Boil the potatoes for 10–15 minutes, or until well cooked. Drain and reserve 500 ml/2 cups of the cooking liquid. Mash the potatoes, then add the reserved cooking liquid, rye flakes and rye flour to form a soft mixture. Let rest in a warm place for 3 hours.

Mix together the yeast and 50 ml/¼ cup lukewarm water. Pour this and 2 tablespoons of the bread flour into the bowl with the rested potato mixture. Mix well. Cover with a clean dish towel and prove in a warm place overnight.

The next day, add the syrup, salt, cumin and enough of the remaining bread flour to make a firm dough. Knead on a lightly floured surface for 10 minutes, then divide into two and shape into round loaves. Place each loaf on a prepared baking sheet. Cover with the dish towel again and let prove in a warm place for 30 minutes. Preheat the oven to 200°C (400°F) Gas 6.

Bake in the preheated oven for 50–60 minutes, or until golden brown. The bread keeps well for 2–3 days.

See photographs on pages 22 and 23

Christmas bread with orange, fennel and raisins

This pretty loaf of bread is slightly sweet and the ideal partner to baked ham at Christmas time. At other times of year, serve it with a cheeseboard; it marries particularly well with milder cheeses, such as Jarlsberg and young Brie.

500 ml/2¼ cups buttermilk

14 g/2 envelopes
(4½ teaspoons) easy-blend/
active dried yeast

3 tablespoons golden syrup
or pure maple syrup

grated zest of 1 unwaxed
orange

1 teaspoon fennel seeds,
freshly ground

½ tablespoon sea salt

200 g/1½ cups wholemeal/
dark rye flour

500 g/3⅔ cups strong white
bread flour

40 g/¼ cup raisins

To finish

1 egg, lightly beaten

a handful of blanched
almonds

*2 baking sheets, lined with
baking parchment*

Makes 2 loaves

Heat the buttermilk in a small saucepan until lukewarm. Whisk in the yeast and syrup, remove from the heat and let stand for 5 minutes.

Transfer the buttermilk mixture to a large mixing bowl and stir in the orange zest, ground fennel and salt. Start adding the flours, first by whisking and then, when the mixture gets too stiff, with a wooden spoon. When all the flour has been added, you should have a firm dough. Cover with a clean dish towel and let prove in a warm place for 30 minutes.

After 30 minutes, knead the raisins into the dough. Divide the dough into two and shape into round loaves. Place each loaf on a prepared baking sheet. Cover with the dish towel again and let rest in a warm place for 30 minutes.

Preheat the oven to 200°C (400°F) Gas 6.

Brush the surface of the loaves with the beaten egg and press the almonds gently into the dough to make a pretty pattern. Bake in the preheated oven for 40 minutes, but if the bread looks well browned after about 30 minutes, lower the temperature to 150°C (300°F) Gas 2 for the last few minutes.

Rye crispbreads

These thin crispbreads are very easy to prepare and ready in minutes. They are wonderfully versatile, so you can either serve them simply with cheese or butter, for breakfast, or as an accompaniment to soups and salads. Sometimes we make them in sticks and serve them as party food with dips like hoummus. They taste great straight out of the oven, but you can let them dry out and store them in an airtight container for several weeks. You can also vary the recipe by adding a little cumin to the dough.

250 g/2 cups strong white bread flour

200 g/1¾ cups wholemeal/dark rye flour

1 teaspoon sea salt

100 g/6½ tablespoons unsalted butter, chilled and cubed

200 ml/¾ cup milk

2 baking sheets, lined with baking parchment

Makes about 64 small crispbreads

Preheat the oven to 230°C (450°F) Gas 8.

Put the flours and salt in a mixing bowl and mix well. Add the cubed butter and rub in using your fingertips until the mixture looks like fine breadcrumbs.

Gradually add the milk to the flour mixture, stirring with a round-bladed knife until a dough forms.

Turn the dough out onto a lightly floured surface and divide into four. Roll out one portion of the dough very thinly with a rolling pin (and cover the other portions with clingfilm/plastic wrap to prevent them from drying out). Cut into about 16 rough shapes (about 9 x 5 cm/3½ x 2 inches) and place on a prepared baking sheet. Prick a few holes in the dough with a fork. Bake in the preheated oven for 4–5 minutes, or until starting to brown in parts. Be careful as it burns very easily.

Repeat with the rest of the dough and bake as above.

Barley flatbreads

These flatbreads are really quick and easy to make – this is 'fast food' at its best! Eat them any way you like. We love them straight out of the oven when a pat of butter melts invitingly on top. You can also eat them with honey, or top them with Jarlsberg cheese or honey-roast ham.

225 g/1¾ cups barley flour

1 teaspoon sea salt

200 ml/¾ cup very cold water

a baking sheet, lined with baking parchment

Makes 4

Preheat the oven to 240°C (475°F) Gas 9.

Mix the flour and salt together in a mixing bowl. Add the cold water and mix quickly into a firm dough. The colder the dough, the better.

Divide the dough into four, and roll into balls between your hands. Place on the prepared baking sheet and flatten with your hands or a floured rolling pin until about 12 cm/4½ inches in diameter and 5 mm/¼ inch thick. Bake in the preheated oven for 15 minutes, or until nicely brown.

LEFT Barley Flatbreads

Rye pockets

When baked, these little breads puff up and become hollow, perfect for filling.

1 tablespoon honey

100 ml/⅓ cup boiling water

150 ml/⅔ cup milk

50 g/3 cakes fresh yeast or 14 g/2 envelopes (4½ teaspoons) easy-blend/active dried yeast

1 teaspoon sea salt

25 g/¼ cup rye flakes

150 g/1 generous cup wholemeal/dark rye flour

50 g/½ cup barley flour

200 g/1½ cups strong white bread flour

1 teaspoon ground cumin

3 tablespoons sunflower oil

Makes 18

Put the honey and water in a large bowl and stir. Add the milk. Crumble the yeast into the warm liquid, then add the salt, rye flakes and rye and barley flours and whisk to combine. Add the bread flour and cumin and mix with a wooden spoon. Add the oil and knead in until smooth. Cover with a clean dish towel and let prove in a warm place for 30–60 minutes, until doubled in size.

Preheat the oven to 240°C (475°F) Gas 9 and put a baking sheet in to heat up.

Pull off pieces of dough the size of plums and roll into balls. Place on sheets of baking parchment to fit the baking sheets and flatten with your hands or a rolling pin to make discs about 5 mm/¼ inch thick. Cover with dish towels and prove in a warm place for 10–15 minutes.

Slide one sheet of baking parchment onto the hot sheet (you will need to bake in batches) and bake at the top of the oven for 10 minutes. The bread will rise and brown well. These are best eaten when freshly baked.

See photographs on pages 30 and 31

Potato and barley flatbreads

This soft flatbread is a great alternative to white bread. It has a distinctive barley taste and a better texture than most sliced white bread. Serve it warm with butter and a mild cheese or ham, or try it alongside a decadent cooked breakfast. You can even make a larger version and eat it as a wrap filled with thinly sliced cucumber and smoked salmon.

400 g/14 oz. floury/baking potatoes, peeled and cut into small chunks

1 teaspoon sea salt

2 tablespoons unsalted butter

250 g/2 cups barley flour

2 baking sheets, lined with baking parchment

Makes about 20

Preheat the oven to 240°C (475°F) Gas 9.

Boil the potatoes for 10–15 minutes, or until tender. Drain, let cool and reserve 200 ml/¾ cup of the cooking liquid.

Add the salt and butter to the potatoes with most of the reserved cooking liquid. Mash to make a smooth, soft mixture. Set aside to cool down a little.

Add the flour to the cooled potato mixture – you should have a firm but pliable dough. Add a little more of the reserved cooking liquid if the dough is too stiff.

Pull off pieces of dough about the size of plums, and roll into balls between your hands. Place on a prepared baking sheet and flatten with your hands or a floured rolling pin to make thin discs. Prick all over with a fork. You will need to bake the flatbreads in batches because they will not all fit on the baking sheets.

Bake in the preheated oven for 15 minutes, or until golden brown with some darker patches.

Parsnip and sesame flatbreads

We tend to bake double portions of these flatbreads, as half of them inevitably disappear as soon as they come out of the oven. Those that survive we serve with a steaming bowl of soup or a meaty stew.

200 g/6½ oz. parsnips, peeled and finely grated

250 g/8 oz. (1 cup) quark/pot cheese (or thick Greek yogurt if necessary)

3 tablespoons rapeseed/canola oil (or vegetable oil)

1 tablespoon golden syrup or pure maple syrup

½ teaspoon sea salt

1 teaspoon bicarbonate of/baking soda

150 g/1¼ cups strong wholemeal/whole-wheat bread flour

150 g/1 cup strong white bread flour

1 egg, lightly beaten, for glazing

sesame seeds, for topping

2 baking sheets, lined with baking parchment

Makes about 14–16

Preheat the oven to 225°C (425°F) Gas 7.

Put the grated parsnip in a saucepan with 100 ml/½ cup water. Bring to the boil, then simmer gently for 5 minutes, or until the parsnip is cooked. Transfer (without draining) to a mixing bowl and set aside to cool.

Add the rest of the ingredients and 100 ml/½ cup water to the mixing bowl and mix to a fairly soft dough.

Drop rounded tablespoons of dough onto the prepared baking sheets, spacing them apart slightly. Sprinkle flour on your hands and flatten the flatbreads until they are about 7 cm/3 inches across. Brush the beaten egg over the flatbreads, to glaze them, and sprinkle sesame seeds over the top.

Bake in the preheated oven for about 10 minutes, or until golden brown. Serve hot or cold.

Savoury pastries

Pastries

All these pastry doughs are used at some point in the following recipes as a base for tarts and quiches, as well as for grissini-type snacks. We use baking powder in them to make them light and slightly doughy. If the pastry is wetter than you are used to, don't worry – this is normal. Make sure your hands and work surface are well floured before starting to handle the pastry. The colder the dough, the easier it is to handle.

Pastry with crème fraîche or sour cream

Use this pastry for the Quiche with Smoked Fish (page 48) and Bacon and Potato Tart (page 52).

200 g/13 tablespoons unsalted butter, softened at room temperature

50 ml/3½ tablespoons crème fraîche or sour cream

150 g/1 generous cup strong white bread flour

1 teaspoon baking powder

a pinch of salt

Cream the butter and crème fraîche or sour cream in a mixing bowl.

In a separate bowl, mix the flour, baking powder and salt. Tip into the mixing bowl and mix until a dough forms.

Roll into a ball, then flatten into a disc before wrapping in clingfilm/plastic wrap. Refrigerate for at least 2 hours, or overnight if possible.

Pastry with quark

Use this pastry for the Salmon Coulibiac (page 44), Vegetable and Blue Cheese Tart (page 47) and Anchovy Twists (page 56). Quark is a popular dairy product in Nordic cuisine, particularly in desserts and baking, and is high in protein and very low in fat.

250 g/2 sticks unsalted butter, softened at room temperature

250 g/1 cup quark cheese

250 g/2 cups strong white bread flour

1 teaspoon baking powder

a pinch of salt

Put the butter and quark in a mixing bowl and beat together with a wooden spoon until well mixed.

In a separate bowl, mix the flour, baking powder and salt together. Tip into the mixing bowl and mix until a dough forms.

Roll into a ball, then flatten into a disc before wrapping in clingfilm/plastic wrap. Refrigerate for at least 30 minutes before continuing with the recipe you are following.

Pastry with cream cheese

Use this pastry for the Minced Meat Pie (page 43).

200 g/13 tablespoons unsalted butter, softened at room temperature

200 g/1 scant cup cream cheese

250 g/2 cups strong white bread flour

1 teaspoon baking powder

a pinch of salt

Put the butter and cream cheese in a mixing bowl and beat together with a wooden spoon until well mixed.

In a separate bowl, mix the flour, baking powder and salt together. Tip into the mixing bowl and mix until a dough forms.

Roll into a ball, then flatten into a disc before wrapping in clingfilm/plastic wrap. Refrigerate for at least 30 minutes before continuing with the recipe you are following.

Pastry with cheddar

Use this pastry for the Wild Mushroom Tart (page 51).

100 g/6½ tablespoons unsalted butter, softened at room temperature

50 g/3 tablespoons crème fraîche or sour cream

50 g/½ cup grated Cheddar

150 g/1¼ cups strong white bread flour

1 teaspoon baking powder

a pinch of salt

Put the butter and crème fraîche or sour cream in a mixing bowl and beat together with a wooden spoon until well mixed.

In a separate bowl, mix the Cheddar, flour, baking powder and salt together. Tip into the mixing bowl and mix until a dough forms.

Roll into a ball, then flatten into a disc before wrapping in clingfilm/plastic wrap. Refrigerate for at least 30 minutes before continuing with the recipe you are following.

Egg-rice pockets

These little pasties are quite filling, and because they're mildly flavoured, they work well with simple soups. We also like serving them at parties or for dinner with a side salad and a beer. These are also suitable for freezing so that you always have a quick snack to hand. Defrost and reheat in the oven until piping hot before serving.

225 g/1¾ cups strong white bread flour

200 g/13 tablespoons unsalted butter, chilled and cubed

75 ml/⅓ cup very cold water

Filling

75 g/½ cup short-grain rice (pudding rice)

2 eggs, plus 1 extra, lightly beaten, for glazing

35 g/2 tablespoons unsalted butter, melted

sea salt and freshly ground black pepper

a round cookie cutter (or an upturned cup), about 10 cm/ 4 inches in diameter

1–2 baking sheets, lined with baking parchment

Makes 16–20

Put the flour in a mixing bowl. Add the cubed butter and rub in using your fingertips until the mixture looks like fine breadcrumbs.

Gradually add the water to the flour mixture, stirring with a round-bladed knife until a dough forms. Wrap in clingfilm/plastic wrap and let rest in the refrigerator for at least for 2 hours, or overnight if possible.

To make the filling, cook the rice according to the manufacturer's instructions. When the rice is ready, it should be quite sticky. Set aside to cool while you make the rest of the filling.

Meanwhile, put the eggs in a small saucepan of cold water and bring to a gentle boil. Simmer for 6–7 minutes, until just hard. Transfer to a bowl of cold water and immerse until the eggs are cool enough to handle. Peel and chop them finely, then mix with the melted butter and cooked rice. Season with salt and black pepper to taste. Set aside.

Preheat the oven to 220°C (425°F) Gas 7.

Take the pastry out of the refrigerator and remove the clingfilm/plastic wrap. Roll the pastry out on a lightly floured surface, with a rolling pin, until about 3 mm/⅛ inch thick. It may be quite sticky, so you might need to dust more flour on the work surface.

Use the cookie cutter to cut out rounds from the pastry. Gather up the offcuts of pastry and refrigerate them briefly before rolling out and cutting out more rounds.

Drop a generous tablespoon of filling onto each pastry round. Fold in half to make a semi-circle and encase the filling. Using your fingers, pinch the edges together to seal the pockets. Arrange the pockets on the prepared baking sheets.

Brush the beaten egg over the pockets with a pastry brush, to glaze them, then prick the top of each one once with a fork. Bake in the preheated oven for about 15 minutes, or until golden brown. Serve hot or cold.

Minced meat pie

Cross-country skiing competitions at school have left a lasting memory, not because of the arduous effort of the skiing involved, but because of the lovely meat pie my mum used to pack for lunch. Every country must have its own version of meat pie with varying types of pastry and filling, and this is the Finnish version. We like using half beef and half pork, minced/ground by the butcher, for the best moist filling, but you may prefer to use just beef, which is also fine. Serve it with a herb salad.

1 quantity Pastry with Cream Cheese (page 39)

Filling

100 g/generous ½ cup short-grain rice (pudding rice)

½ vegetable or beef stock cube

2 tablespoons rapeseed/canola oil (or vegetable oil)

1 large onion, finely chopped

300 g/10 oz. minced/ground beef and/or pork

1½ teaspoons ground paprika

½ teaspoon ground cayenne pepper

sea salt and freshly ground black pepper or white pepper

1 egg, lightly beaten, for glazing

a baking sheet, lined with baking parchment

Serves 6 as a starter/appetizer or 4 as a main course/entrée

Make the Pastry with Cream Cheese according to the recipe on page 39 but divide it into two before wrapping each portion in clingfilm/plastic wrap.

To make the filling, cook the rice according to the manufacturer's instructions, but crumble the stock cube into the saucepan before starting. When the rice is ready, it should be quite sticky. Set aside to cool while you make the rest of the filling.

Heat 1 tablespoon of the oil in a frying pan and fry the onion until soft and golden. Remove the onion from the pan with a slotted spoon and set aside to cool in a mixing bowl.

Put the remaining oil in the frying pan and fry the meat, stirring often, until cooked and evenly browned. Season with the paprika, cayenne pepper and salt and black or white pepper, to taste. Set aside to cool.

When everything has cooled down slightly, mix it all in the mixing bowl.

Preheat the oven to 200°C (400°F) Gas 6.

Take the pastry out of the refrigerator and remove the clingfilm/plastic wrap. Roll one portion out on a lightly floured surface, with a rolling pin, into a rectangle about 30 x 25 cm/12 x 10 inches. Repeat with the other portion. Gently and loosely roll one rectangle around the rolling pin and transfer it to the prepared baking sheet for the base of the pie. Spoon the filling evenly over the surface, leaving a 2-cm/1-inch border. Brush the border with beaten egg.

Roll the second rectangle of pastry around the rolling pin and lay it neatly over the pie filling. Seal the edges by pressing the pastry between your thumb and forefinger at regular intervals along the edge. Brush the rest of the beaten egg over the pie lid and prick it in a few places with a fork. Very lightly score diagonal lines across the top. Bake in the preheated oven for 25 minutes, or until golden brown. Serve warm or cold. It will keep in the refrigerator for 2 days.

Salmon coulibiac

This dish is of Russian origin. It's a very good option for a relaxed dinner party because it looks so attractive when sliced, and you can make it in advance. We like to serve it as a starter with some rocket/arugula and cherry tomatoes.

1 quantity Pastry with Quark (page 38)

Filling

180 g/1 cup short-grain rice (pudding rice)

4 eggs, plus 1 extra, lightly beaten, for glazing

1 quantity Gravad Lax (page 12, but brush the topping away before using in this recipe)

a small handful of fresh dill, chopped

sea salt and freshly ground black pepper

a baking sheet, lined with baking parchment

Serves 8–10

Make the Pastry with Quark according to the recipe on page 38 but divide it into two before wrapping each portion in clingfilm/plastic wrap.

To make the filling, cook the rice according to the manufacturer's instructions. When the rice is ready, it should be quite sticky. Set aside to cool. Meanwhile, put the eggs in a small saucepan of cold water and bring to a gentle boil. Simmer for 6–7 minutes, until just hard. Transfer to a bowl of cold water and immerse until the eggs are cool enough to handle. Peel and slice about 1.5 cm/⅗ inch thick.

Preheat the oven to 220°C (425°F) Gas 7.

Place the gravad lax, skin-side down, on a board. Using a sharp knife, cut into the fish diagonally, starting from the thicker part. When the knife hits the skin, turn the knife flat to make a short cut along the skin. Pull out the knife and repeat this process 2 cm/¾ inch further along. A slice of gravad lax should come away, leaving the skin behind. Continue with the remaining gravad lax, setting the slices aside as you go.

Take the pastry out of the refrigerator and remove the clingfilm/plastic wrap. Roll one portion out on a lightly floured surface, with a rolling pin, into a rectangle about 30 x 25 cm/12 x 10 inches. Repeat with the other portion. Gently and loosely roll one rectangle around the rolling pin and transfer it to the prepared baking sheet for the base of the pie. Spread the cooled rice evenly over the surface, leaving a 2-cm/1-inch border. Lay the slices of gravad lax flat on top of the rice, down the length of the pastry. Overlap the slices, if you need to, to use them all up. Sprinkle the dill, then the eggs over the top. Brush the border with beaten egg.

Roll the second rectangle of pastry around the rolling pin and lay it neatly over the pie filling. The pastry should encase the filling snugly, so cut off any excess dough and set aside. Seal the edges by pressing the pastry between your thumb and forefinger at regular intervals along the edge. Brush more of the beaten egg over the pie lid. Cut the reserved dough into long, thin strips and lay over the pie in a criss-cross pattern. Brush the rest of the beaten egg over the strips. Prick the pie in a few places with a fork. Bake in the preheated oven for 20–25 minutes, or until golden brown. Serve warm or cold. Keeps in the refrigerator for 2 days.

Vegetable and blue cheese tart

The Danes and the Finns each have their own type of blue cheese. It's a popular ingredient in cooking, from salads and pastas to pies. Here's a summer favourite with broccoli and cauliflower, but you can vary the recipe by using your own favourite vegetables – make sure you don't use vegetables that become watery when cooked, or that take a particularly long time to cook.

½ quantity Pastry with Quark (page 38)

Filling

200 g/1½ cups broccoli florets

200 g/1½ cups cauliflower florets

1 tablespoon rapeseed oil (or vegetable oil)

1 onion, chopped

100 g/1 cup cherry tomatoes, halved

75 g/2½ oz. Danish blue cheese, Finnish Aura, or any crumbly blue cheese, crumbled

75 g/¾ cup grated Cheddar

freshly ground black pepper

a 26-cm/10-inch loose-bottomed, fluted tart pan, greased

Serves 6 as a starter/ appetizer or 4 as a main course/entrée

Make the Pastry with Quark according to the recipe on page 38.

Preheat the oven to 200°C (400°F) Gas 6.

Cut the broccoli and cauliflower florets into chunks slightly larger than cherry tomatoes. Boil until al dente, then drain and set aside to cool.

Heat the oil in a frying pan and fry the onion until soft and golden. Set aside to cool slightly.

Take the pastry out of the refrigerator and remove the clingfilm/plastic wrap. Roll the pastry out on a lightly floured surface, with a rolling pin, until it is slightly larger than the tart pan. Gently and loosely roll the pastry around the rolling pin and transfer it to the prepared tart pan. Line the pan with the pastry, pressing it into the fluted edges of the pan and neatly cutting off the excess pastry.

Tip the onion and any remaining oil from the pan into the pastry case and spread evenly. Top with the broccoli, cauliflower and cherry tomatoes. Sprinkle the cheeses evenly over the top and season with black pepper.

Bake in the preheated oven for 25 minutes, or until golden brown. Serve warm or cold.

Quiche with smoked fish

It's typical of Nordic cooking to feature fish of some kind. We like haddock in this quiche, but you can replace it with any smoked fish, such as cold smoked salmon. Serve the quiche hot or warm, with a green salad.

1 quantity Pastry with Crème Fraîche or Sour Cream (page 38)

Filling

1 tablespoon rapeseed/canola oil (or vegetable oil)

2 leeks, trimmed, cleaned and thinly sliced

3 eggs

150 ml/⅔ cup single/light cream

100 g/1 cup grated Cheddar

a small handful of fresh dill, finely chopped

200 g/6½ oz. smoked fish (e.g. smoked haddock), boned and cut into 1-cm/½-inch cubes

sea salt and freshly ground black pepper

a 26-cm/10-inch loose-bottomed, fluted tart pan, greased

Serves 6–8

Make the Pastry with Crème Fraîche or Sour Cream according to the recipe on page 38.

Preheat the oven to 200°C (400°F) Gas 6.

Take the pastry out of the refrigerator and let soften for a few minutes while you make the filling. Do not let it come to room temperature, as it is easier to handle when cold.

To make the filling, heat the oil in a frying pan over low–medium heat. Stir in the leeks and cook for a few minutes until nearly soft. Set aside.

Put the eggs, cream, Cheddar and dill in a mixing bowl and season with salt and black pepper. Mix well.

Remove the clingfilm/plastic wrap from the pastry. Roll the pastry out on a lightly floured surface, with a rolling pin, until it is slightly larger than the tart pan. Gently and loosely roll the pastry around the rolling pin and transfer it to the prepared tart pan. Line the pan with the pastry, pressing it into the fluted edges of the pan and neatly cutting off the excess pastry.

Sprinkle the leek and smoked fish into the pastry case, then pour the cream mixture on top. If you have some dough left over, cut thin ribbons from it and arrange them on top of the quiche.

Bake in the preheated oven for 25–30 minutes, or until the pastry is golden brown.

Wild mushroom tart

We Nordic people live from the forest, so mushrooms play an important part in our cuisine. The mushroom season starts with morels in June, followed by chanterelles in July and August, and we can find porcini mushrooms all through the autumn. If you know your mushrooms and can forage for your own, use those, but the ones featured in this recipe can all be found in a well-stocked supermarket.

1 quantity Pastry with Cheddar (page 39)

Filling

30 g/1 oz. dried porcini mushrooms

30 g/2 tablespoons unsalted butter

1 onion, chopped

1 garlic clove, crushed

300 g/10 oz. mixed fresh mushrooms (e.g. portabellini, chestnut, cremini, button mushrooms), sliced

250 g/1 cup crème fraîche or sour cream

3 eggs, lightly beaten

2 tablespoons snipped fresh chives

100 g/1 cup grated Cheddar

½ teaspoon sea salt

freshly ground black pepper

a 28-cm/11-inch loose-bottomed, fluted tart pan, greased

Serves 6–8

Make the Pastry with Cheddar according to the recipe on page 39.

Preheat the oven to 200°C (400°F) Gas 6.

Put the dried porcini mushrooms in a small bowl and just cover with boiling water. Let soak for 20 minutes. Drain, rinse and chop.

Melt the butter in a frying pan over medium heat and fry the onion, garlic and fresh mushrooms for 3–5 minutes, until the onions and garlic are turning golden and the mushrooms have lost most of their moisture. Drain off any excess moisture, then set aside to cool.

Put the crème fraîche, eggs, chives, Cheddar, salt and some black pepper in a mixing bowl and mix well. Add the cooked mushroom mixture and the chopped porcini mushrooms and stir well.

Take the pastry out of the refrigerator and remove the clingfilm/plastic wrap. Roll the pastry out on a lightly floured surface, with a rolling pin, until it is slightly larger than the tart pan. Gently and loosely roll the pastry around the rolling pin and transfer it to the prepared tart pan. Line the pan with the pastry, pressing it into the fluted edges of the pan and neatly cutting off the excess pastry. Tip the mushroom mixture into the pastry case and spread evenly.

Bake in the preheated oven for about 30 minutes, or until the filling is firm and golden brown. Serve warm or cold.

Bacon and potato tart

This recipe is traditionally made with smoked reindeer, but since reindeer meat is not widely available around the world, we have replaced it with bacon. You could also use pastrami or salt beef.

1 quantity Pastry with Crème Fraîche or Sour Cream (page 38)

500 g/1 lb. small waxy potatoes

1 tablespoon vegetable oil

120 g/4 oz. streaky/thick-sliced bacon

2 celery stalks, finely chopped

100 ml/6 tablespoons crème fraîche or sour cream

2 tablespoons horseradish sauce

1 tablespoon rapeseed/canola oil (or vegetable oil)

a small handful of fresh flat leaf parsley, chopped

a 26-cm/10-inch loose-bottomed, fluted tart pan, greased

Serves 6–8

Make the Pastry with Crème Fraîche or Sour Cream according to the recipe on page 38.

Preheat the oven to 200°C (400°F) Gas 6.

Boil the potatoes until tender. Drain and let cool slightly, then peel off the skins and cut into 1-cm/½-inch thick slices. Peeling and slicing potatoes only after cooking ensures that they do not disintegrate when boiled.

Take the pastry out of the refrigerator and let soften for a few minutes while you make the filling. Do not let it come to room temperature, as it is easier to handle when cold.

Heat the vegetable oil in a frying pan and fry the bacon for a couple of minutes until nicely cooked. Remove from the pan with a slotted spoon and let cool slightly, then roughly chop.

Meanwhile, fry the celery in the same frying pan until softened. Remove from the heat and let cool slightly.

Mix the crème fraîche and horseradish sauce together.

Remove the clingfilm/plastic wrap from the pastry. Roll the pastry out on a lightly floured surface, with a rolling pin, until it is slightly larger than the tart pan. Gently and loosely roll the pastry around the rolling pin and transfer it to the prepared tart pan. Line the pan with the pastry, pressing it into the fluted edges of the pan and neatly cutting off the excess pastry.

Brush the pastry case with the rapeseed/canola oil. Arrange the sliced potatoes over the base of the tart, then add the bacon, celery and parsley. Finally, dollop the crème fraîche mixture on top.

Bake in the preheated oven for 20 minutes, or until the bacon looks crispy and the pastry is golden brown. Serve warm or cold.

Karelian pies

These little pies are an old favourite in Finland, sold everywhere in supermarkets and becoming increasingly popular at our Nordic Bakery stores. The contrast between the wheat-free rye crust and the soft rice filling is unusual, but addictive. The thinner the crust, the better the pie. It's often served with a mixture of softened butter and chopped, hardboiled egg on top.

250 g/2 cups wholemeal/dark rye flour

1 teaspoon sea salt

1 tablespoon rapeseed/canola oil (or vegetable oil)

plain/all-purpose flour, for dusting

75 g/5 tablespoons unsalted butter, melted

Filling

150 g/¾ cup short-grain rice (pudding rice)

750 ml/3 cups milk

1 teaspoon sea salt

Topping (optional)

1 egg, hardboiled

40 g/2½ tablespoons unsalted butter, softened at room temperature

1–2 baking sheets, lined with baking parchment

Makes 20

To make the filling, put 250 ml/1 cup water in a saucepan and bring to the boil. Add the rice and simmer for 5–10 minutes. Add the milk and continue to simmer over low heat for 30–40 minutes, until the rice is cooked and you have a thickened rice pudding consistency. Stir in the salt and set aside to cool while you make the pastry.

Preheat the oven to 220°C (425°F) Gas 7.

Put the rye flour and salt in a mixing bowl, add the oil and gradually add 200 ml/¾ cup water, mixing with a round-bladed knife or by hand until a dough is formed. Transfer the dough to a surface lightly floured with plain/all-purpose flour and shape into a long sausage shape. Divide into 20 pieces and roll each one into a ball. Using a rolling pin, roll each ball into thin rounds, about 10 cm/4 inches in diameter.

Put 2 tablespoons of the filling in the middle of each round, leaving about 2 cm/¾ inch around the edge. Lift up the edge of the pastry around the filling to make an oval, open pie. Pinch the pastry between your thumb and forefinger along the edge and make sure that the edge is standing up and encasing the filling.

Pour the melted butter into a medium bowl. You want to be able to fit a wooden spoon inside it to submerge it in butter. Now put one pie on the spoon and dip it into the bowl to coat just the pastry crust generously in butter. Put the pie on a prepared baking sheet and repeat with the remaining pies.

Bake in the preheated oven for 15–20 minutes, until golden brown and crispy round the edges.

The traditional way to serve the pies is with an egg-butter mixture, which can be prepared in advance. Chop the hardboiled egg and mix with the butter and a pinch of salt. Serve with the pies, for spooning on top.

Anchovy twists

The Pastry with Quark (page 38) used in the Salmon Coulibiac makes a great base for all kinds of little snacks. You can sprinkle grated Cheddar over the pastry dough and twist it into cheese straws, or you can use the simple anchovy filling below. These twists make a lovely party snack or accompaniment to pre-dinner drinks, soups and salads.

1 quantity Pastry with Quark (page 38)

1 egg, lightly beaten, for glazing

60 g/2 oz. anchovy fillets in oil, drained and finely chopped

a baking sheet, lined with baking parchment

Makes 20–25

Make the Pastry with Quark according to the recipe on page 38 but divide it into two before wrapping each portion in clingfilm/plastic wrap.

Preheat the oven to 220°C (425°F) Gas 7.

Take the pastry out of the refrigerator and remove the clingfilm/plastic wrap. Roll one portion out on a lightly floured surface, with a rolling pin, into a rectangle about 40 x 30 cm/16 x 12 inches. Repeat with the other portion. Brush some of the egg over each portion of pastry. Divide the chopped anchovies in two and spread them evenly over half of each pastry rectangle.

Fold the bare pastry half over the anchovy filling and press gently together. Repeat with the other pastry rectangle. Brush the remaining beaten egg over the top. Cut into strips about 1 cm/½ inch wide and twist each strip into a spiral. Arrange on the prepared baking sheet.

Bake in the preheated oven for 7–9 minutes, or until golden brown. Serve warm or cold.

Cakes

Tiger cake

This cake gets its name from the tiger stripes formed by the two colours of cake mixture – vanilla and chocolate. It's really a marble cake, but we like to call it a tiger cake! It's particularly attractive when baked in a bundt pan, so do try to get hold of one if you can.

300 g/2¾ sticks unsalted butter, softened at room temperature

250 g/1¼ cups (caster) sugar

3 teaspoons vanilla extract

5 eggs

3 teaspoons baking powder

300 g/2⅓ cups plain/all-purpose flour

2 tablespoons cocoa powder

2 tablespoons double/heavy cream

a 23-cm/9-inch bundt pan or 18-cm/7-inch springform cake pan, greased

Makes 12–16 slices

Preheat the oven to 180°C (350°F) Gas 4.

Put the butter and sugar in a large mixing bowl and cream with a wooden spoon or handheld electric whisk until pale and fluffy. Stir in the vanilla extract. Add the eggs one by one, whisking well after each addition.

In a separate bowl, sift the baking powder and flour together, then fold into the egg mixture.

Spoon about one-third of the mixture into a separate bowl and fold in the cocoa powder and cream.

Spoon 2 tablespoons of plain mixture into the prepared cake pan, then 1 tablespoon of chocolate mixture. Alternate in this way until you have run out of mixture and the two colours are spread randomly through the cake pan. Level the top with the back of the spoon.

Bake in the preheated oven for 50–60 minutes, until the cake is firm to the touch and a skewer inserted in the centre comes out clean.

Tiger cake keeps for several days in an airtight container. We also think it tastes better a day or two after baking.

Orange and poppy seed cake

This delicious cake is lightly blended with nutty poppy seeds and the tangy taste of orange. The recipe makes a generously-sized cake and keeps well, so it's perfect for baking on a lazy weekend and tucking into throughout the week with a cup of tea.

300 g/2¾ sticks unsalted butter, softened at room temperature

250 g/1¼ cups (caster) sugar

3 teaspoons vanilla extract

5 eggs

3 teaspoons baking powder

300 g/2⅓ cups plain/all-purpose flour

grated zest of 1½ unwaxed oranges (if you can't find unwaxed, scrub the peel with a scourer to remove the wax or use organic oranges)

freshly squeezed juice of ½ orange

1 tablespoon poppy seeds

an 18-cm/7-inch springform cake pan, greased

Makes 12–16 slices

Preheat the oven to 180°C (350°F) Gas 4.

Put the butter and sugar in a large mixing bowl and cream with a wooden spoon or handheld electric whisk until pale and fluffy. Stir in the vanilla extract. Add the eggs one by one, whisking well after each addition.

In a separate bowl, sift the baking powder and flour together, then fold into the egg mixture.

Fold in the orange zest, juice and poppy seeds until well mixed.

Spoon the mixture into the prepared cake pan and level the top with the back of the spoon.

Bake in the preheated oven for 50–60 minutes, until the cake is firm to the touch and a skewer inserted into the centre comes out clean. The cake tastes best the day after baking and is also suitable for freezing.

Ginger cake

This recipe is deliciously aromatic, with a lovely texture. If you can't find ground cloves, you can use whole ones and then grind them as finely as possible with a pestle and mortar or in a spice mill.

300 g/2¾ sticks unsalted butter, softened at room temperature

250 g/1¼ cups light muscovado/packed light brown sugar

3 teaspoons vanilla extract

5 eggs

3 teaspoons baking powder

1½ teaspoons ground cinnamon

1½ teaspoons ground cloves

3 teaspoons cardamom seeds, crushed with a pestle and mortar

1½ teaspoons ground ginger

300 g/2⅓ cups plain/all-purpose flour

an 18-cm/7-inch springform cake pan, greased

Makes 12–16 slices

Preheat the oven to 180°C (350°F) Gas 4.

Put the butter and sugar in a large mixing bowl and cream with a wooden spoon or handheld electric whisk until pale and fluffy. Stir in the vanilla extract. Add the eggs one by one, whisking well after each addition.

In a separate bowl, sift the baking powder, spices and flour together, then fold into the egg mixture.

Spoon the mixture into the prepared cake pan and level the top with the back of the spoon.

Bake in the preheated oven for 50–60 minutes, until the cake is firm to the touch and a skewer inserted into the centre comes out clean. The cake tastes best the day after baking and is also suitable for freezing.

Banana cake

Everyone loves banana bread, or cake, as we call it. Ours is packed with the spices that typify Nordic baking: ginger, cardamom and cinnamon. Throw in some ground cloves and really ripe bananas and you have a delicious and very easy cake for any time of day.

150 g/10 tablespoons
unsalted butter, softened
at room temperature

250 g/1¼ cups (caster) sugar

2 eggs

2 teaspoons baking powder

1 teaspoon salt

1 teaspoon ground ginger

2 teaspoons cardamom
seeds, crushed with a pestle
and mortar

2 teaspoons ground
cinnamon

1 teaspoon ground cloves

300 g/2⅓ cups plain/
all-purpose flour

5 ripe bananas, mashed

a 23-cm/9-inch bundt pan
or 22-cm/8-inch springform
cake pan, greased

Makes 12–16 slices

Preheat the oven to 180°C (350°F) Gas 4.

Put the butter and sugar in a large mixing bowl and mix well. Add the eggs one by one, whisking well after each addition.

In a separate bowl, sift the baking powder, salt, spices and flour together, then fold into the egg mixture.

Finally, add the mashed bananas and mix well.

Spoon the mixture into the prepared cake pan and level the top with the back of the spoon.

Bake in the preheated oven for 1 hour and 20 minutes, or until a skewer inserted into the centre comes out clean. The cake tastes even better a day or two after baking and is also suitable for freezing.

Spice cake with dates and rye

Rich fruit cakes aren't a traditional feature of Scandinavian baking, but this dark cake is probably as close as we get to it. It's rich with dates and spices, while the rye flour gives it a nice, slightly nutty flavour.

175 g/1½ cups chopped pitted dates

freshly squeezed juice of 1 lemon

200 g/13 tablespoons unsalted butter, softened at room temperature

225 g/1 generous cup light muscovado/packed light brown sugar

½ teaspoon vanilla extract

2 eggs

1 teaspoon bicarbonate of/baking soda

1 teaspoon ground cinnamon

2 teaspoons cardamom seeds, crushed with a pestle and mortar

200 g/1⅔ cups wholemeal/dark rye flour

an 18-cm/7-inch springform cake pan, greased and dusted with flour

Makes 12–16 slices

Put the dates and 200 ml/¾ cup water in a small saucepan over low heat. Simmer for about 10 minutes, or until well softened. Stir in the lemon juice and mix well until it resembles a paste. Set aside to cool.

Preheat the oven to 170°C (325°F) Gas 3.

Put the butter and sugar in a large mixing bowl and cream with a handheld electric whisk until fluffy and the colour of pale toffee. Stir in the vanilla extract. Add the eggs one at a time, whisking well after each addition.

In a separate bowl, sift the bicarbonate of/baking soda, spices and flour together, then fold into the egg mixture. Add the date mixture and fold in until well combined.

Spoon the mixture into the prepared cake pan and level the top with the back of the spoon.

Bake in the preheated oven for 50 minutes, or until a skewer inserted into the centre comes out clean. Let cool for 15 minutes before removing the cake from the pan.

Birthday cake with cream and berries

This is a cake recipe I learned from my grandmother who used to bake it every year at our summer house. Not only is it easy to scale up and down, it's very versatile because you can layer it with the filling of your choice. Take three equal-sized glasses. Allow half an egg per person, and break the correct number of eggs into the first glass. Pour enough sugar into the second glass to come to the same level as the eggs. Repeat with flour in the third glass. This way you always get the correct proportions even if the size of the eggs varies. You can bake the cake a day in advance and fill and decorate it on the day of serving.

4 eggs, at room temperature

225 g/1 generous cup (caster) sugar

1 teaspoon baking powder

170 g/1⅓ cups self-raising flour

Filling

500 ml/2 cups whipping cream

vanilla sugar or icing/confectioners' sugar, to taste and for dusting (optional)

300 ml/1¼ cups apple juice

your choice of fruit (e.g. strawberries, blueberries, blackberries, sliced bananas, chopped kiwi fruit, canned pineapple pieces)

2 loose-bottomed cake pans, 26 cm/10 inches in diameter, greased

Serves 8–10

Preheat the oven to 200°C (400°F) Gas 6.

Put the eggs and sugar in a large mixing bowl and whisk with a handheld electric whisk until the mixture is foam-like – this will take up to 10 minutes. When it is ready, it will be almost white, have doubled in size and the batter will drop off the beaters in a figure-of-eight when you lift them out of the bowl.

In a separate bowl, sift the baking powder and flour together, then fold into the egg mixture as gently and briefly as possible – do not overwork the mixture otherwise it will lose its fluffiness.

Divide the mixture between the prepared cake pans. Bake in the preheated oven for 35–40 minutes, until the cakes are golden brown and a skewer inserted into the centre of each comes out clean. Let cool while you make the filling.

Whip the cream until soft peaks form. Add vanilla sugar or icing/confectioners' sugar to taste, if you like.

Remove the cooled cakes from their pans. Cut each one horizontally through the middle to make two equal layers. Lay one layer on a cake stand. Sprinkle one-quarter of the apple juice evenly over the cake layer to moisten it. Spread one-quarter of the whipped cream over it, followed by one-quarter of your choice of fruit. Repeat this process four times, finishing with a decorative assortment of fruit on top. Dust lightly with vanilla sugar or icing/confectioners' sugar and serve.

Oatbake with blueberries and raspberries

This is our favourite dessert for a weekend brunch. The fresh berries make it irresistible and not too heavy. Serve it with a dollop of whipped cream or a helping of custard if you think it needs a little something else.

100 g/¾ cup rolled (porridge) oats

300 ml/1¼ cups hot milk

100 g/6½ tablespoons unsalted butter, softened at room temperature

60 g/5 tablespoons (caster) sugar

50 ml/3 tablespoons (runny) honey

1 teaspoon vanilla extract

1 egg, lightly beaten

1 teaspoon baking powder

120 g/1 cup plain/all-purpose flour

150 g/1 generous cup blueberries

150 g/1 generous cup raspberries

icing/confectioners' sugar, for dusting

a 900-g/2-lb. loaf pan, greased

Serves 6

Preheat the oven to 180°C (350°F) Gas 4.

Put the oats and hot milk in a mixing bowl and set aside for a few minutes to allow the oats to absorb most of the milk and to cool down slightly.

Put the butter and sugar in a separate bowl and cream with a wooden spoon or handheld electric whisk until pale and fluffy. Stir in the honey and vanilla extract. Gradually add the egg, a little at a time, beating well after each addition.

Sift the baking powder and flour together, then fold into the butter mixture. Drain any remaining liquid from the oats, then stir into the mixing bowl.

Pour the mixture into the prepared loaf pan and sprinkle the blueberries and raspberries evenly on top.

Bake in the preheated oven for 50–60 minutes, until a skewer inserted into the centre comes out clean. Let rest in the pan for 10 minutes before turning out onto a wire rack to cool. Dust with a little icing/confectioners' sugar before serving.

Tosca cake

The crunchy almond topping makes this simple classic one of Sweden's best-loved cakes, perfect with afternoon tea or as a dessert with a dollop of cream.

4 eggs

170 g/generous ¾ cup (caster) sugar

200 ml/generous ¾ cup double/heavy cream

100 g/6½ tablespoons unsalted butter, melted and cooled

2 teaspoons vanilla extract

2 teaspoons baking powder

260 g/2 cups plain/ all-purpose flour

Tosca topping

75 g/5 tablespoons unsalted butter

75 g/⅓ cup (caster) sugar

50 ml/3 tablespoons double/ heavy cream

3 tablespoons plain/ all-purpose flour

75 g/¾ cup flaked/slivered almonds

a 29-cm/11-inch springform cake pan, greased

Serves 6–8

Preheat the oven to 200°C (400°F) Gas 6.

Put the eggs and sugar in a large mixing bowl and whisk with a handheld electric whisk until the mixture is foam-like – this will take up to 10 minutes. When it is ready, it will be almost white, have doubled in size and the batter will drop off the beaters in a figure-of-eight when you lift them out of the bowl.

Add the cream, melted butter and vanilla extract, and fold in gently.

In a separate bowl, sift the baking powder and flour together, then fold into the egg mixture.

Pour the mixture into the prepared cake pan and bake in the preheated oven for 30–35 minutes.

While the cake is baking, make the Tosca topping. Put all ingredients in a saucepan over low heat, stir to mix and bring gently to the boil.

Remove the baked cake from the oven, spread the Tosca topping evenly over it and return to the hot oven for a further 10–15 minutes, or until the topping is golden and slightly caramelized.

Toffee layer cake

This classic cake is made for special occasions and summer celebrations. The toffee topping originates from Russia and works brilliantly with the cream and the soft, feather-light cake crumb.

4 eggs

200 g/1 cup golden caster/raw cane sugar

1 teaspoon baking powder

75 g/generous ½ cup plain/all-purpose flour

50 g/6 tablespoons cornflour/cornstarch

2 tablespoons orange juice or milk

2 tablespoons apricot jam or apple compote

To decorate

400 ml/1⅔ cups whipping cream

100 g/½ cup golden caster/raw cane sugar

1½ tablespoons unsalted butter

a 22-cm/8-inch springform cake pan, greased

Makes 8–10 slices

Preheat the oven to 180°C (350°F) Gas 4.

Put the eggs and sugar in a large mixing bowl and whisk with a handheld electric whisk until the mixture is foam-like – this will take up to 10 minutes. When it is ready, it will be very pale, have doubled in size and the batter will drop off the beaters in a figure-of-eight when you lift them out of the bowl.

In a separate bowl, sift the baking powder and flours together, then fold into the egg mixture.

Spoon the mixture into the prepared cake pan and bake in the preheated oven for 30–40 minutes, until a skewer inserted into the centre comes out clean. Let rest in the pan for 10 minutes before turning out onto a wire rack to cool for a further 20 minutes.

To decorate, whip half the whipping cream until quite firm.

Cut the cake horizontally through the middle to make two equal layers. Lay one layer on a cake stand and sprinkle half the orange juice or milk over it to moisten it. It is best to start from the edge and work towards the centre. Spread the apricot jam or apple compote evenly on top, then spread half the whipped cream over that. Place the second layer of cake on top, then sprinkle the remaining juice or milk over it.

To make a toffee icing, put the sugar and remaining unwhipped cream in a saucepan and bring to the boil. Simmer over low heat for 10 minutes, or until it thickens. Add the butter and stir until melted and smooth. Pour the toffee over the cake, using a spatula dipped in hot water to spread it evenly, if necessary. Spread the remaining whipped cream neatly over the side of the cake. Refrigerate the cake for at least 1 hour before serving, to allow the toffee to set.

Arctic roll with vanilla and chocolate

This is a classic from the 1970s and we think it deserves a comeback. We love it as a dessert both in the summer and the winter. Serve it on its own or with custard or hot chocolate sauce on the side.

3 eggs

100 g/½ cup (caster) sugar

2 teaspoons baking powder

30 g/¼ cup cornflour/cornstarch

2 tablespoons cocoa powder

50 g/⅓ cup icing/confectioners' sugar

Filling

1 litre/quart vanilla ice cream

50 g/2 oz. dark/bittersweet chocolate, grated

a large baking sheet, lined with baking parchment

Serves 6–8

Preheat the oven to 200°C (400°F) Gas 6.

Put the eggs and sugar in a large mixing bowl and whisk with a handheld electric whisk until the mixture is foam-like – this will take up to 10 minutes. When it is ready, it will be almost white, have doubled in size and the batter will drop off the beaters in a figure-of-eight when you lift them out of the bowl.

In a separate bowl, sift the baking powder, cornflour/cornstarch and cocoa powder together, then fold into the egg mixture.

Spread the mixture evenly on the prepared baking sheet with a spatula to make a rough square about 30 x 30 cm/12 x 12 inches in size. (The mixture will not spread when it bakes.) Bake in the preheated oven for 10 minutes.

In the meantime, take the ice cream for the filling out of the freezer to soften for about 10 minutes.

Cut a sheet of baking parchment slightly bigger than the baked cake, lay it on the work surface and dust generously with some of the icing/confectioners' sugar. Carefully lift the hot, baked cake from the baking sheet, using the lining baking parchment and place it face down on the dusted baking parchment. Gently peel the lining baking parchment away from the cake and let cool for a few minutes.

Spread the softened ice cream over the cake, scatter the grated chocolate evenly over it, then roll it carefully into a log shape. Freeze for at least 1 hour.

Before serving, trim the ends of the roll, let stand for 15 minutes to soften, then dust with more icing/confectioners' sugar.

Carrot and rye muffins with blueberries

We love these little carrot cakes. They're like muffins, but a much healthier alternative because they're made with rye flour and sweetened with a small amount of brown sugar, molasses, carrots and dried blueberries. Nevertheless, they're very tasty, in our opinion!

50 g/¼ cup packed dark brown soft sugar

2 tablespoons molasses

3 tablespoons boiling water

150 g/1 generous cup wholemeal/dark rye flour

½ teaspoon bicarbonate of/ baking soda

2 teaspoons baking powder

1 teaspoon ground cinnamon

1 teaspoon ground ginger

½ teaspoon ground allspice

40 g/⅓ cup desiccated coconut

40 g/⅓ cup dried blueberries (or raisins)

1 egg, beaten

3 tablespoons sunflower oil

2 medium carrots, finely grated

a 12-hole muffin pan, lined with paper cases

Makes 12

Preheat the oven to 180°C (350°F) Gas 4.

Put the sugar, molasses and boiling water in a small heatproof bowl and stir to dissolve. Set aside to cool down a little.

In a separate, large mixing bowl, mix the flour, bicarbonate of/baking soda, baking powder, spices, coconut and blueberries together. Add the beaten egg, oil, grated carrots and sugar mixture and mix briefly until just incorporated.

Divide the mixture between the paper cases and bake in the preheated oven for 20–25 minutes, or until risen and browned.

Cinnamon bun

Pastries and buns

Classic cinnamon buns

This is one of Nordic Bakery's bestselling products and perfectly encapsulates the flavours of Finnish baking. Try one of these hearty buns for breakfast or any time of day with coffee, tea or hot chocolate. When baked, the top should be firm, with a soft interior of cinnamon, sugar and butter. Delicious!

Dough

570 ml/2⅓ cups lukewarm milk

150 g/¾ cup (caster) sugar

45 g/3 cakes fresh yeast or 14 g/2 envelopes (4½ teaspoons) easy-blend/active dried yeast

1 teaspoon cardamom seeds, crushed with a pestle and mortar

180 g/1½ sticks unsalted butter, melted

1 egg

1 kg/8 cups plain/all-purpose flour

Filling

100 g/6½ tablespoons unsalted butter, softened at room temperature

200 g/1 cup packed dark brown soft sugar

3 tablespoons ground cinnamon

Glaze

85 g/scant ½ cup (caster) sugar

1 tablespoon freshly squeezed lemon juice

2 baking sheets, lined with baking parchment

Makes 12–13

To make the dough, put the milk, sugar, yeast, cardamom, melted butter and egg in a food processor or mixer with a dough hook. With the motor running, gradually add the flour until it is all incorporated and the dough has come together.

Transfer the dough to a bowl, cover with a clean dish towel and let prove in a warm place for 1 hour, or until it has doubled in size.

After 1 hour, punch down the dough and transfer to a lightly floured surface. Using a rolling pin, roll it out until it is about 30 x 80 cm/12 x 31 inches and 7 mm/¼ inch thick.

For the filling, spread the butter evenly over the dough and sprinkle the sugar and cinnamon all over the top.

Roll the dough up from a long side. Cut into roughly 6-cm/2½-inch rolls, but cut them at an angle – so, make the first cut diagonally, then the second cut about 6 cm/2½ inches along diagonally in the opposite direction. You should get a roll that looks like a trapezium (or a triangle with the tip chopped off). Carefully transfer the buns to the prepared baking sheets, with the longest edge of the bun sitting on the sheet, cover with dish towels again and let prove in a warm place for 30–60 minutes, until almost doubled in size.

Preheat the oven to 200°C (400°F) Gas 6.

Bake the buns in the preheated oven for 20–25 minutes, or until golden brown.

To make the glaze, put the sugar, lemon juice and 100 ml/½ cup water in a small saucepan and bring to the boil. Simmer for 10–15 minutes, until slightly thickened. The glaze will still be quite watery.

Remove the buns from the oven, transfer to a wire rack and brush the glaze generously over them. Let cool before serving.

Boston cake

This is a festive version of the Classic Cinnamon Buns on the previous page, but they are packed tightly into a round cake pan so that they look like a cake when they come out of the oven. They should be pulled apart and enjoyed individually while still warm. As for why this is called a Boston Cake – it's a mystery! At the Bakery, we tend to sprinkle flaked/slivered almonds over the top before baking, and then cut the cake into slices. See the end of the recipe for this variation.

½ quantity Classic Cinnamon Buns dough (page 85, but follow the method here; you will have ½ egg left over but reserve that for glazing)

(caster) sugar, for sprinkling

Filling

50 g/3½ tablespoons unsalted butter, softened at room temperature

100 g/½ cup packed dark brown soft sugar

1½ tablespoons ground cinnamon

a 25-cm/10-inch round cake pan, greased

Makes 8–9

Follow the recipe on page 85 to make half the quantity of dough. After the first proving, punch down the dough and transfer to a lightly floured work surface. Using a rolling pin, roll it out until it is about 30 x 40 cm/ 12 x 16 inches and 1 cm/½ inch thick.

For the filling, spread the butter evenly over the dough and sprinkle the sugar and cinnamon all over the top.

Roll the dough up from a long side, then cut into roughly 4-cm/1¾-inch rolls. Arrange the rolls, cut-side down, in the prepared cake pan. They should fit quite snugly.

Preheat the oven to 200°C (400°F) Gas 6.

Cover with the dish towel again and let prove in a warm place for 15 minutes.

Lightly beat the reserved ½ egg. Brush the tops of the buns with the beaten egg and sprinkle with (caster) sugar. Bake the cake in the preheated oven for 25 minutes, or until golden brown.

Remove from the oven and let cool in the pan for 10 minutes before tipping out onto a wire rack.

Variation: If you like, you can sprinkle 75 g/¾ cup flaked/slivered almonds on top of the buns before baking. When baked and slightly cooled, remove from the pan and cut into slices to serve. See photograph on page 58.

Soft cinnamon buns

This is an old-fashioned alternative to the classic buns on page 85. We found this recipe in an old notebook from our school home economy lessons. Making the dough in two stages gives it that extra-soft texture that we love. They are best eaten fresh from the oven.

Stage 1

25 g/1½ cakes fresh yeast or 7 g/1 envelope (2¼ teaspoons) easy-blend/active dried yeast

200 ml/generous ¾ cup lukewarm milk

1 teaspoon (caster) sugar

130 g/1 cup strong white bread flour

Stage 2

65 g/⅓ cup (caster) sugar

½ teaspoon salt

1 teaspoon cardamom seeds, crushed with a pestle and mortar

75 g/5 tablespoons unsalted butter, melted

260 g/2 cups strong white bread flour

Filling and glazing

25 g/2 tablespoons unsalted butter, softened at room temperature

3 tablespoons demerara sugar

2 tablespoons ground cinnamon

1 egg, lightly beaten, for glazing

(caster) sugar, for sprinkling

2–3 baking sheets, lined with baking parchment

Makes about 24

For Stage 1, crumble the yeast into the milk in a large mixing bowl. Whisk in the sugar and flour. Set aside for about 10 minutes, or until slightly bubbly.

For Stage 2, add the sugar, salt, cardamom and melted butter to the mixing bowl. Mix well. Add the flour and mix until you have a dough, then knead on a lightly floured surface for 10–15 minutes, until the dough is no longer sticky.

Return the dough to the bowl, cover with a clean dish towel and let prove in a warm place for 30 minutes, or until it has doubled in size.

Punch down the dough and knead on the lightly floured surface until firm. Divide the dough into two. Roll one portion out, with a rolling pin, into a rectangle about 30 x 50 cm/12 x 20 inches. Repeat with the other portion.

For the filling, spread the butter evenly over both portions of pastry and sprinkle the demerara sugar and cinnamon all over the tops.

Roll the pastry up from a long side. Cut into roughly 4-cm/1¾-inch rolls and place on the prepared baking sheets, flattening them slightly with your hand. Cover with the dish towel again and let prove in a warm place for 30 minutes.

Preheat the oven to 200°C (400°F) Gas 6.

To glaze, brush the tops of the buns with the beaten egg and sprinkle with (caster) sugar. Bake the buns in the preheated oven for about 10–12 minutes, or until golden brown.

Sweet tosca bread

We love the sweet and crunchy almond topping from the Tosca Cake on page 75 so much that we like to use it in various ways. It is perfect on this large, flat bun, which has a lovely milky dough and is lighter than Tosca Cake. In Finnish, it is called "pannupulla", which translates as "bun-in-a-pan". It is best eaten freshly baked, with a hot drink or a glass of milk.

250 ml/1 cup milk

50 g/3 tablespoons unsalted butter

7 g/1 envelope (2¼ teaspoons) easy-blend/active dried yeast

2 teaspoons cardamom seeds, crushed with a pestle and mortar

450 g/3½ cups strong white bread flour

85 g/scant ½ cup (caster) sugar

½ teaspoon salt

Tosca topping

3 tablespoons milk

50 g/3 tablespoons unsalted butter

50 g/¼ cup packed light brown soft sugar

50 g/½ cup flaked/slivered almonds

a baking sheet, lined with baking parchment

Makes 8 good slices

Heat 100 ml/½ cup of the milk in a large saucepan. When hot, add the butter and stir until melted. Transfer to a large mixing bowl and stir in the rest of the milk so that the liquid is lukewarm.

In a separate bowl, mix the yeast, cardamom and flour together.

Whisk the sugar and salt into the mixing bowl. Start adding the flour mixture, first by whisking and then, when the mixture gets too stiff, with a wooden spoon. When all the flour has been added, you should have a firm dough.

Transfer the dough to a lightly floured surface and knead for 10 minutes, or until the dough is no longer sticky. Add a little more flour, if necessary. Return the dough to the bowl, cover with a clean dish towel and let prove in a warm place for 1 hour.

Preheat the oven to 200°C (400°F) Gas 6.

While the dough is proving, make the Tosca topping. Heat the milk in a small saucepan, then add the butter and sugar and bring to the boil. Lower the heat and simmer for a few minutes. Stir in the almonds.

Punch down the dough and knead it on a lightly floured surface for a few seconds. Shape into a ball, put it on the prepared baking sheet, then flatten it into a round or rough square about 28 cm/11 inches across. (Butter or oil your hands if the dough feels sticky.) Spread the topping evenly over the top. Bake in the preheated oven for 20 minutes, or until nicely browned.

Pulla bread

This is a traditional recipe for a popular sweet bread similar to brioche but softer and sweeter. Cut into slices or tear off chunks and enjoy still warm from the oven. Delicious at breakfast with coffee, it's also good the following day – toast it and top it with butter and jam or honey.

30 g/1½ cakes fresh yeast or 7 g/1 envelope (2¼ teaspoons) easy-blend/active dried yeast

250 ml/1 cup lukewarm milk

½ teaspoon salt

100 g/½ cup (caster) sugar, plus extra for sprinkling

1 tablespoon cardamom seeds, crushed with a pestle and mortar

2 eggs, lightly beaten

700 g/5½ cups strong white bread flour

100 g/6½ tablespoons unsalted butter, softened at room temperature

50 g/⅓ cup raisins

30 g/⅓ cup flaked/slivered almonds

a baking sheet, lined with baking parchment

Serves 8

Crumble the yeast into the milk in a large mixing bowl. Whisk in the salt, sugar, cardamom and three-quarters of the eggs.

Add a little of the flour and whisk well to introduce lots of air into the dough. Add the rest of the flour, then the butter and knead everything together with your hands until the dough is firm and no longer sticky.

Cover the bowl with a clean dish towel and let prove in a warm place for 30 minutes, or until the dough has doubled in size.

Preheat the oven to 200°C (400°F) Gas 6.

After 30 minutes, punch down the dough and knead the raisins into it on a lightly floured surface. Divide the dough into three and roll each piece into a rope about 50 cm/20 inches long. Each rope should be the same length. Line up the ropes side by side on the prepared baking sheet and attach them together at one end by pressing the dough together. Plait the ropes, and finish by pressing the ends together. Fold and tuck both ends of the pulla underneath to neaten it.

Brush the tops of the pulla with the remaining beaten egg and sprinkle the almonds and some (caster) sugar over the top. Bake in the preheated oven for 25–30 minutes, or until golden brown.

Little butter buns

These little buns are firm family favourites. Young children can roll out the little balls of dough themselves and fill with a dollop of sweetened butter. They can then decorate the buns with colourful sugar sprinkles, if they like.

250 ml/1 cup milk

1 egg, lightly beaten

85 g/scant ½ cup (caster) sugar

1 teaspoon salt

2 teaspoons cardamom seeds, crushed with a pestle and mortar

7 g/1 envelope (2¼ teaspoons) easy-blend/active dried yeast

500 g/4 cups strong white bread flour

75 g/5 tablespoons unsalted butter, softened at room temperature

sugar sprinkles, to decorate (optional)

Filling and glazing

50 g/3 tablespoons unsalted butter, softened at room temperature

3 tablespoons (caster) sugar

1 egg, lightly beaten

1–2 baking sheets, lined with baking parchment

Makes 20

Heat the milk in a large saucepan until lukewarm. Whisk the egg with a little of the warm milk, then pour into the pan and whisk. Add the sugar, salt and cardamom to the pan and mix well.

Mix the yeast and flour together. Add a little of the flour mixture to the saucepan and whisk well to introduce lots of air into the dough. Continue to add the flour mixture, first by whisking and then, when the mixture gets too stiff, with a wooden spoon. Finally, add the butter and knead it into the dough with your hands until thoroughly incorporated.

Transfer the dough to a lightly floured surface and knead for 10 minutes, or until the dough is elastic and no longer sticky. Add a little more flour, if necessary. Return the dough to the bowl, cover with a clean dish towel and let prove in a warm place for 1 hour, or until doubled in size.

After 1 hour, punch down the dough and knead it on the floured surface again for a few minutes. Divide it into four, then divide each piece into five again, so that you end up with 20 pieces. Roll each into a ball between your hands and arrange on the prepared baking sheets. Cover with dish towels again and let prove in a warm place for 30 minutes.

Meanwhile, to make the filling, mix the butter and sugar together.

Preheat the oven to 200°C (400°F) Gas 6.

After 30 minutes, press your finger into the top of each bun to make a hole, and fill with about ½ teaspoon of the filling. Brush the beaten egg over the top and sprinkle with sprinkles, if you like. Bake in the preheated oven for 10 minutes, or until golden.

Almond twists

These use the same dough as in the previous little buns, but the twisted form gives a nice, different texture. Instead of ground almonds, you can also use a cinnamon and sugar mix in the filling.

250 ml/1 cup milk, lukewarm

1 egg, lightly beaten

85 g/scant ½ cup (caster) sugar

1 teaspoon salt

2 teaspoons cardamom seeds, crushed with a pestle and mortar

7 g/1 envelope (2¼ teaspoons) easy-blend/active dried yeast

500 g/4 cups strong white bread flour

75 g/5 tablespoons unsalted butter, softened at room temperature

20 g/¼ cup flaked/slivered almonds

Filling and glazing

25 g/⅛ cup ground almonds

2 tablespoons (caster) sugar

50 g/2 tablespoons unsalted butter, softened at room temperature

1 egg, lightly beaten

1–2 baking sheets, lined with baking parchment

Makes about 15

Heat the milk in a large saucepan until lukewarm. Whisk the egg with a little of the warm milk, then pour into the pan and whisk. Add the sugar, salt and cardamom to the pan and mix well.

Mix the yeast and flour together. Add a little of the flour mixture to the saucepan and whisk well to introduce lots of air into the dough. Continue to add the flour mixture, first by whisking and then, when the mixture gets too stiff, with a wooden spoon. Finally, add the butter and knead it into the dough with your hands until thoroughly incorporated.

Transfer the dough to a lightly floured surface and knead for 10 minutes, or until the dough is elastic and no longer sticky. Add a little more flour, if necessary. Return the dough to the bowl, cover with a clean dish towel and let rise in a warm place for 1 hour, or until doubled in size.

Meanwhile, to make the filling, mix the almonds and sugar together.

Preheat the oven to 200°C (400°F) Gas 6.

After 1 hour, punch down the dough and knead it on the floured surface again for a few minutes. Using a rolling pin, roll it out until it is about 30 x 50 cm/12 x 20 inches.

For the filling, spread the butter over the dough. Scatter the almond mixture over one half of the rectangle (i.e. an area of 30 x 25 cm/12 x 10 inches on one side). Fold the bare pastry half over the filling and press gently together. Place the rectangle, now measuring 30 x 25 cm/ 12 x 10 inches, horizontally in front of you. Using a sharp knife, cut the pastry into 25-cm/10-inch long and 2-cm/¾-inch wide strips. Hold a strip between your fingers and twist in opposite directions, then roughly coil it in on itself like a snail and press the ends together underneath. Arrange on the prepared baking sheets, cover with dish towels again and let prove in a warm place for another 10 minutes.

Brush the beaten egg over the top and sprinkle with the flaked/slivered almonds. Bake in the preheated oven for 10 minutes, or until golden.

Dough sticks

This is a different and fun way to bake simple bread – wrap the dough around a skewer and bake on a barbecue, campfire or in the oven. It's a great idea for barbecue buffets or cookouts. Eat freshly baked just on their own or with jam.

200 g/1½ cups strong white bread flour

½ teaspoon salt

2 tablespoons (caster) sugar

7 g/1 envelope (2¼ teaspoons) easy-blend/active dried yeast

150 ml/⅔ cup lukewarm milk or water

1 tablespoon vegetable oil

8 bamboo skewers

Makes 8

Soak the bamboo skewers in cold water for at least 20 minutes while you make the dough.

Put the flour, salt, sugar and yeast in a mixing bowl and stir well to mix. Make a well in the middle and pour the milk or water, and oil into it. Mix well to form a firm dough. Transfer the dough to a lightly floured surface and knead for 5 minutes. Return the dough to the bowl, cover with a clean dish towel and let prove in a warm place for 30 minutes.

Prepare a barbecue/grill or preheat the oven to 200°C (400°F) Gas 6.

After 30 minutes, punch down the dough and transfer to the floured surface. Divide it into eight, then roll each piece into a thin rope. Each rope should be the same length. Wrap each rope tightly around a bamboo skewer, pressing the ends down well to ensure that the dough does not come apart while baking.

Bake the dough sticks over the barbecue/grill or in the preheated oven for 10 minutes, or until risen and golden, turning over frequently.

Soft cheese and pineapple buns

These buns are a summer favourite at the Bakery. Quark is a relatively uncommon cheese, but you should be able to find it in most large supermarkets. The white quark filling makes a lovely contrast to the golden brown of the baked bun and will look inviting in any breakfast basket.

Dough

7 g/1 envelope (2¼ teaspoons) easy-blend/active dried yeast

250 ml/1 cup lukewarm milk

1 egg, lightly beaten

85 g/scant ½ cup (caster) sugar

2 teaspoons cardamom seeds, crushed with a pestle and mortar

500 g/4 cups plain/all-purpose flour

100 g/6½ tablespoons unsalted butter, melted

1 egg, lightly beaten, for brushing

Filling

2 eggs

170 g/6½ oz. (⅔ cup) quark/pot cheese

130 g/½ cup Greek yogurt

220 g/7 oz. canned pineapple in fruit juice, drained and finely chopped

2 tablespoons (runny) honey

2 tablespoons (caster) sugar

2 teaspoons vanilla sugar or vanilla extract

1–2 baking sheets, lined with baking parchment

Makes 20

To make the dough, sprinkle the yeast into the warm milk in a large mixing bowl and whisk until the yeast has dissolved. Add the egg, sugar, cardamom and two-thirds of the flour and mix well until you have a soft dough. Add the rest of the flour with the melted butter and knead for a couple of minutes.

Cover the bowl with a clean dish towel and let prove in a warm place for 30–60 minutes, or until the dough has doubled in size.

After 30–60 minutes, punch down the dough and transfer to a lightly floured work surface. Divide it into four, then divide each piece into five again, so that you end up with 20 pieces. Roll each into a ball between your hands and arrange on the prepared baking sheets. If the dough is too sticky to handle, add a little more flour. Press your finger into the middle of each bun to make a deep hole. Cover with dish towels again and let prove in a warm place for 30 minutes.

Meanwhile, to make the filling, mix all the ingredients together.

Preheat the oven to 180°C (350°F) Gas 4.

After 30 minutes, spoon the filling into the hole in the buns. (You may need to rework the holes if they have filled in while the buns were proving.) Brush the remaining beaten egg around the sides and bake in the preheated oven for 15–20 minutes, or until golden.

Christmas star pastries

These are beautiful cakes we traditionally make around Christmas time. They are really very simple to create, but so pretty with a dollop of plum jam in the centre.

1 quantity Pastry with Quark
(page 38)

150 g/⅔ cup plum jam
or marmalade

1 egg, lightly beaten,
for glazing

*a baking sheet, lined with
baking parchment*

Makes about 10

Make the Pastry with Quark according to the recipe on page 38 but divide it into two before wrapping each portion in clingfilm/plastic wrap.

Preheat the oven to 220°C (425°F) Gas 7.

Take the pastry out of the refrigerator and remove the clingfilm/plastic wrap. Roll one portion out on a lightly floured surface, with a rolling pin, until it is about 5 mm/¼ inch thick. Cut out 10-cm/4-inch squares with a sharp knife. Re-roll any offcuts to make more squares and repeat with the second portion of dough. For each square, cut a 2.5-cm/1-inch line from each corner towards the centre.

Drop a teaspoon of jam into the very centre of each square.

Pull a corner into the centre and press down gently. Repeat with the remaining corners, so that you have a star shape, and stick the tips of the pastry together with a dab of water.

When you have done this with all the pastries, brush the beaten egg over them and bake in the preheated oven for 8 minutes, or until golden brown. Let cool under a clean dish towel. The pastries will keep in an airtight container for 2 days.

Nest cakes

These fritters are called "tippaleipä" in Finnish and are eaten on May Day to celebrate the coming of spring. You don't have to save them up for the occasion though – they are equally good as a special dessert, drizzled with melted chocolate.

3 eggs

a pinch of salt

40 g/3 tablespoons (caster) sugar

150 ml/⅝ cup milk

½ teaspoon vanilla extract

200 g/1½ cups plain/all-purpose flour

sunflower oil, for shallow frying

icing/confectioners' sugar, for dusting

a frying pan, at least 20 cm/8 inches in diameter

a piping bag, fitted with a plain, medium nozzle/tip, or a strong freezer bag with a corner snipped off

an 8–10-cm/3–4-inch cookie cutter or rösti ring

Makes about 18

Put the eggs, salt, (caster) sugar, milk, vanilla extract and flour in a mixing bowl and whisk until well combined. Let stand for 30 minutes.

Pour enough sunflower oil into the frying pan to make a depth of 2 cm/1 inch. (It is important that the oil is not too deep in the pan; you are shallow frying here, so the batter should be able to sit on the base of the pan, not float to the top of the oil in loose strands.) Heat the oil until a blob of batter dropped into the oil sizzles and browns after a few seconds. If it browns too quickly, lower the heat under the pan.

Place the cookie cutter or rösti ring into the oil.

Fill the piping bag with about a cupful of the batter. (You will need to make the cakes in batches.) Hold the bag over the cookie cutter and pipe batter into it to form a nest shape, filling it no deeper that the cutter itself. When the batter looks like it is starting to set, remove the cookie cutter with tongs.

Cook the cake for 1 minute, then flip over. When golden brown on both sides, remove carefully and leave on kitchen paper/paper towels to absorb any oil while you make the rest of the cakes. Let cool for a little while, then dust with icing/confectioners' sugar and let set.

Cardamom doughnuts

These irresistible little doughnuts are fried in hot oil, so be very careful when you're making them, especially if children are helping. We use cardamom to give them that distinctive Nordic flavour.

75 g/5 tablespoons unsalted butter

300 ml/1¼ cups milk

2 eggs, lightly beaten

½ teaspoon salt

85 g/scant ½ cup (caster) sugar

2 teaspoons cardamom seeds, crushed with a pestle and mortar

7 g/1 envelope (2¼ teaspoons) easy-blend/active dried yeast

500 g/4 cups strong white bread flour

sunflower oil, for deep-frying

icing/confectioners' sugar, for dusting

Makes 22

Melt the butter in a large saucepan, then take the pan off the heat. Add the milk, eggs, salt, (caster) sugar, and cardamom.

In a bowl, mix the yeast and flour together. Tip into the saucepan and mix until you get a nice, soft dough. Cover with a clean dish towel and let prove in a warm place for 1 hour.

After 1 hour, punch down the dough and knead it briefly on a lightly floured surface. Divide it into two, then divide each piece into 11, so that you end up with 22 pieces. Roll each into a ball between your hands, cover with dish towels again and let prove for another 30 minutes.

Pour enough sunflower oil into a large, deep frying pan to make a depth of 5–7 cm/2–3 inches. Heat the oil until a cube of bread dropped into the oil sizzles and browns within a few seconds.

Drop a few doughnuts into the hot oil very carefully – the number you can fry in one go will depend on the size of the pan. Deep-fry each doughnut until golden brown underneath, then turn over with tongs and fry the other side until golden brown. To check if it is cooked through, cut one in half. If it still looks raw, lower the temperature of the hob and return the doughnut to the hot oil until cooked.

Remove each cooked doughnut carefully and leave on kitchen paper/paper towels to absorb any oil while you fry the rest. Let cool for a little while, then dust with icing/confectioners' sugar.

Tarts and cookies

Blueberry tart with rye

The Nordic forests are full of blueberries in the summer, so they feature in many pies and desserts. Like the Summer Berry Lattice Tart on page 116, this is another popular tart, but with a crème fraîche and sour cream topping. It's a simple and attractive option for the end of a casual meal with friends.

100 g/6½ tablespoons unsalted butter, softened at room temperature

85 g/scant ½ cup (caster) sugar

1 egg, lightly beaten

100 g/¾ cup plain/all-purpose flour

60 g/½ cup wholemeal/dark rye flour

1 teaspoon baking powder

Filling

100 g/⅓ cup crème fraîche or double/heavy cream

150 ml/⅔ cup sour cream

1 egg, lightly beaten

3 tablespoons (caster) sugar

1 teaspoon vanilla extract

250 g/1 pint blueberries

a 24-cm/10-inch loose-bottomed, fluted tart pan, greased

Serves 6–8

Preheat the oven to 200°C (400°F) Gas 6.

Put the butter and sugar in a mixing bowl and beat until well mixed. Gradually add the egg, mixing well. Tip in the flours and baking powder and mix again until a dough has formed.

Transfer the dough to the tart pan and push and press it into the pan until the base and sides are evenly covered with a neat layer of dough.

To make the filling, put the crème fraîche, sour cream, egg, sugar and vanilla extract in a mixing bowl and mix well. Pour into the pastry case, then scatter the blueberries into the tart.

Bake in the preheated oven for 25 minutes, or until the filling has set and the pastry is golden brown.

Simple apple tart

Fast to make and tasty to eat, this recipe offers a delicious solution to the glut of apples from our apple tree. A dollop of vanilla ice cream or whipped cream makes it a real treat.

100 g/6½ tablespoons unsalted butter, softened at room temperature

85 g/scant ½ cup (caster) sugar

1 egg, lightly beaten

100 g/¾ cup plain/all-purpose flour

60 g/½ cup wholemeal/dark rye flour

1 teaspoon baking powder

vanilla ice cream or whipped cream, to serve

Filling

2 large cooking apples (about 300 g/10 oz. in weight once peeled and cored), peeled, cored and thinly sliced

1 tablespoon (caster) sugar

1 tablespoon ground cinnamon

a 24-cm/10-inch loose-bottomed, fluted tart pan, greased

Serves 6–8

Preheat the oven to 200°C (400°F) Gas 6.

Put the butter and sugar in a mixing bowl and beat until well mixed. Gradually add the egg, mixing well. Tip in the flours and baking powder and mix again until a dough has formed.

Transfer the dough to the tart pan and push and press it into the pan until the base and sides are evenly covered with a neat layer of dough.

To make the filling, put the sliced apples, sugar and cinnamon in a bowl and mix together until the apples are evenly coated, then transfer to the pastry case and spread roughly, or arrange neatly in a pattern over the base of the tart.

Bake in the preheated oven for 25 minutes, or until golden brown. Remove from the oven, let cool slightly, then serve with vanilla ice cream or whipped cream.

Rhubarb tart

The base for this tart is a lovely cross between pastry and cookie. When you mix the dough, it will feel wet, but that is how it should be – just flour your hands before you press the dough into the tart pan. The rhubarb and oat filling makes the tart moist and very tasty.

150 g/1 generous cup plain/all-purpose flour

1 teaspoon baking powder

100 g/6½ tablespoons unsalted butter, softened at room temperature and diced

85 g/scant ½ cup (caster) sugar

1 egg yolk

Filling

300 g/10 oz. rhubarb, trimmed and roughly chopped

2 tablespoons dark brown soft sugar

50 g/3 tablespoons unsalted butter, softened at room temperature and diced

60 g/⅓ cup (caster) sugar

50 g/scant ½ cup rolled (porridge) oats

a 20-cm/8-inch loose-bottomed, fluted tart pan, greased

Serves 6–8

Preheat the oven to 200°C (400°F) Gas 6.

Sift the flour and baking powder into a mixing bowl. Rub the butter into the flour mixture with your fingertips until it looks like breadcrumbs. Stir in the sugar and egg yolk and mix until a dough forms.

Transfer the dough to the tart pan and push and press it into the pan until the base and sides are evenly covered with a neat layer of dough.

To make the filling, put the rhubarb and brown sugar in a bowl and mix until the rhubarb is evenly coated, then transfer to the pastry case and spread roughly over the base of the tart.

In a separate bowl, mix the butter, (caster) sugar and oats together until you have a rough mixture like a crumble topping. Scatter roughly over the rhubarb filling.

Bake in the preheated oven for 30 minutes, or until the crumble topping and pastry are golden brown.

Summer berry lattice tart

This pretty, rustic tart is traditionally made with wild blueberries, which are smaller and less sweet than the cultivated ones. You can use any blueberries you like or even a mixture of summer berries, which add a little sharpness and contrast with the softness of the pastry.

7 g/1 envelope (2¼ teaspoons) easy-blend/active dried yeast

500 g/4 cups strong white bread flour

250 ml/1 cup lukewarm milk

85 g/scant ½ cup (caster) sugar

½ teaspoon salt

1 egg, lightly beaten

75 g/5 tablespoons unsalted butter, softened at room temperature

icing/confectioners' sugar, for dusting

whipped cream, to serve

Filling

3 tablespoons cornflour/cornstarch

3 tablespoons (caster) sugar

500 g/1 lb. blueberries or a mixture of summer berries (if using frozen berries, defrost them in a sieve/strainer in advance to drain off the excess liquid)

40 g/½ cup dried breadcrumbs

a roasting pan, 23 x 32 cm/ 9 x 13 inches, lined with baking parchment

Serves 6–8

Mix the yeast and flour together in a bowl.

Put the milk, sugar, salt and half the egg in a mixing bowl and whisk together. Tip the flour mixture into the bowl and mix, kneading with your hands when it gets firm. Finally, add the butter and knead it into the dough with your hands until thoroughly incorporated. Cover with a clean dish towel and let prove in a warm place for 30 minutes.

Preheat the oven to 200°C (400°F) Gas 6.

To make the filling, put the cornflour/cornstarch, sugar and berries in a separate bowl and mix until the berries are evenly coated.

Punch down the dough and roll out on a lightly floured surface, with a rolling pin, until it is 4 cm/1¾ inches larger than the prepared roasting pan. (Reserve the pastry offcuts for the lattice topping.) Gently and loosely roll the pastry around the rolling pin and transfer it to the prepared roasting pan. Line the pan with the pastry – the pastry should line the base of the pan and go only slightly up the sides. Neatly cut off the excess pastry.

Sprinkle the breadcrumbs over the pastry case, then spread the berry mixture evenly over the top.

To make the lattice topping, gather up the offcuts of pastry and roll out on the floured work surface again. Cut into long strips and lay four strips diagonally across the top of the tart, trimming the strips to fit. Repeat with four strips in the opposite direction. Stick the ends of the strips to the edge of the tart with a dab of water. Brush the remaining beaten egg over the pastry to glaze.

Bake in the preheated oven for 30 minutes. Let cool slightly, then dust with icing/confectioners' sugar and serve warm with a dollop of whipped cream.

Tartlets with berries and cream

The tartlet cases for this recipe can be made in advance and they keep well in an airtight container for a few days. After filling, the tartlets are best eaten on the same day. Traditionally they are topped with small, wild, forest berries, but for this recipe we have used storebought strawberries and blueberries.

150 g/1 generous cup plain/
all-purpose flour

50 g/⅓ cup icing/
confectioners' sugar

a pinch of salt

50 g/3 tablespoons unsalted
butter, chilled and diced

1 egg, lightly beaten

Filling

300 ml/1¼ cups whipping
cream

2 tablespoons (caster) sugar

½ teaspoon vanilla extract

300 g/1½ cups strawberries,
hulled and quartered if large

150 g/1 cup blueberries

icing/confectioners' sugar,
for dusting

a 12-hole muffin pan

baking beans

Makes about 12

Sift the flour, sugar and salt into a mixing bowl. Rub the butter into the flour mixture with your fingertips until it looks like fine breadcrumbs.

Make a well in the middle and pour the egg into it. Using a spoon, mix the egg quickly into the mixture to form a dough. Roll into a ball, then wrap in clingfilm/plastic wrap and refrigerate for at least 1 hour.

Take the pastry out of the refrigerator and remove the clingfilm/plastic wrap. Roll the pastry out on a lightly floured surface, with a rolling pin, until about 2 mm/¹⁄₁₆ inch thick.

Use a cookie cutter or thin glass to cut out rounds slightly larger than the base of the muffin pan holes. Gather up the offcuts of pastry and roll out and cut out more rounds. Press the pastry rounds into the holes of the muffin pan, then refrigerate the pan for 15 minutes.

Preheat the oven to 180°C (350°F) Gas 4.

Line the tartlet cases with small pieces of baking paper, fill with baking beans and bake blind in the preheated oven for 10 minutes. Remove the beans and paper and bake for a further 3–4 minutes.

Pop the baked tartlet cases gently out of the muffin pan and let cool completely on a wire rack.

To make the filling, whip the cream with the sugar and vanilla extract until soft peaks form. Fill the tartlet cases with a spoonful of the whipped cream, top with the berries and dust with icing/confectioners' sugar.

Miriam's rhubarb meringue pie

My aunt Miriam bakes fantastic pies, and this is one of her – and my – favourites.

100 g/6½ tablespoons unsalted butter, softened

65 g/⅓ cup (caster) sugar

2 eggs, separated

125 g/1 cup plain/all-purpose flour

1 teaspoon baking powder

3 tablespoons milk

Filling

3–4 sticks of rhubarb, trimmed and roughly chopped

1 teaspoon ground cinnamon

65 g/⅓ cup plus 2 teaspoons (caster) sugar

1 teaspoon vanilla extract

50 g/½ cup flaked/slivered almonds

a 24-cm/10-inch loose-bottomed, fluted tart pan, greased

Serves 6–8

Preheat the oven to 180°C (350°F) Gas 4.

Cream the butter and sugar until pale and fluffy. Add the egg yolks one by one, mixing well. Mix the flour and baking powder together, then add half to the butter mixture, mixing well. Add half the milk and mix well. Finally, add the remaining flour mixture, mix, then add the remaining milk and mix well. Transfer the dough to the tart pan and push and press it until the base and sides are evenly covered with a layer of dough. To make the filling, mix the rhubarb, cinnamon and 2 teaspoons of the sugar together, then spread roughly over the tart. Whisk the egg whites until they hold soft peaks, then gradually add the remaining sugar, whisking until firm. Fold in the vanilla extract. Spoon on top of the pie, making peaks as you go, and scatter the almonds over the top. Bake in the preheated oven for 35–40 minutes.

Oven-baked pancakes

Oven-baked pancakes are an everyday treat in Finland, loved by children and adults alike.

100 g/½ cup (caster) sugar

275 g/2 generous cups plain/all-purpose flour

2 teaspoons baking powder

1 teaspoon salt

2 eggs, lightly beaten

800 ml/3⅓ cups milk

1 teaspoon vanilla extract

100 g/6½ tablespoons unsalted butter

icing/confectioners' sugar, for dusting

berries or jam, and whipped cream or ice cream, to serve

a roasting pan, 23 x 32 cm/9 x 13 inches

Makes 8 slices

Combine the sugar, flour, baking powder and salt in a mixing bowl. Make a well in the middle and pour the eggs and a little of the milk into it. Whisk the dry ingredients gradually into the well. When combined, whisk in the remaining milk and the vanilla extract until smooth. Let stand for 30 minutes.

Preheat the oven to 200°C (400°F) Gas 6. Put the butter in the roasting pan and heat in the oven until melted. Take the pan out of the oven and use a pastry brush to brush the melted butter all around the insides of the pan before pouring the excess into the pancake batter. Stir well, then pour all the batter into the roasting pan.

Bake in the hot oven for 30–40 minutes, until golden.

Let cool slightly, then dust with icing/confectioners' sugar, cut into 8 slices and serve with berries or jam and whipped cream or ice cream.

RIGHT Oven-baked Pancakes

For Miriam's Rhubarb Meringue Pie, see photographs on pages 120 and 121

Lace oat cookies with chocolate, raisins and hazelnuts

These unusual cookies will spread into thin, lacy tuiles when baked. They are studded with chunks of white and dark chocolate, and hazelnuts and raisins.

120 g/1 stick unsalted butter, melted

2 tablespoons double/heavy cream

a drizzle of (runny) honey

80 g/scant ½ cup (caster) sugar

80 g/¾ cup rolled (porridge) oats

2 tablespoons plain/ all-purpose flour

30 g/¼ cup raisins

30 g/1 oz. white chocolate, roughly chopped

30 g/1 oz. dark/bittersweet chocolate, roughly chopped

40 g/⅓ cup shelled hazelnuts, chopped

3 baking sheets, lined with baking parchment

Makes 14–16

Preheat the oven to 200°C (400°F) Gas 6.

Put the melted butter, cream and honey in a small bowl and mix well.

In a large mixing bowl, mix the sugar, oats, flour, raisins, chopped chocolate and hazelnuts together. Pour the butter mixture into the bowl and mix well.

Drop 1 tablespoon of the batter per cookie onto the prepared baking sheets, leaving plenty of space between them, as they will spread when they bake. You should allow about 5 cookies per sheet.

Bake in the preheated oven for 5–10 minutes, until golden brown.

Let cool for at least 15 minutes before removing from the sheet because they will set and firm up as they cool.

If you like, you can create shapes before the cookies have cooled by laying them over a cup or a rolling pin and letting them set.

Store for up to 1 week in an airtight container with greaseproof paper between each cookie.

Spoon cookies with raspberry jam

This is the kind of classic cookie you'll find in your grandmother's well thumbed cookbook. Bake a batch of them for a stylish afternoon tea.

200 g/13 tablespoons
unsalted butter

130 g/⅔ cup (caster) sugar

2 teaspoons vanilla sugar
or 1 teaspoon vanilla extract

1 teaspoon baking powder

220 g/1¾ cups plain/
all-purpose flour

about 10 tablespoons
raspberry jam or marmalade

1 teaspoon icing/
confectioners' sugar

*1–2 baking sheets, lined with
baking parchment*

Makes about 10

Preheat the oven to 170°C (325°F) Gas 3.

Put the butter in a small saucepan, melt over low heat, then bring to the boil gently, stirring with a wooden spoon. Remove from the heat when the butter foams and let it settle before pouring it into a mixing bowl.

Add the (caster) sugar and vanilla sugar or extract, to the mixing bowl, mix well and let cool.

In a separate bowl, mix the baking powder and flour together. Tip into the butter mixture and mix until well combined.

Take one teaspoon of dough and place on a prepared baking sheet, using a second teaspoon to help you drop the dough onto the sheet and make it into a neat round. Leave a little space between them, as they may spread when they bake.

Bake the cookies in the preheated oven for 10–14 minutes, until just turning golden.

Let cool a little before transferring the cookies to a wire rack to cool completely. Spoon a tablespoon of jam onto the flat side of a cookie and sandwich with another cookie. Dust with icing/confectioners' sugar just before serving. Store in an airtight container for up to 5 days.

Raspberry twists

These biscuits are very pleasing to look at, served on a tray for an elegant afternoon tea. Raspberry jam works well because of the colour contrast with the cookie dough, but you can use marmalade instead if you prefer.

200 g/13 tablespoons unsalted butter, softened at room temperature

125 g/⅔ cup (caster) sugar

1 egg

1 teaspoon vanilla extract

250 g/2 cups plain/all-purpose flour

1 teaspoon baking powder

150 g/⅔ cup raspberry jam or marmalade

icing/confectioners' sugar, for dusting

2–3 baking sheets, lined with baking parchment

Makes 35–40

Put the butter and sugar in a mixing bowl and cream it with a wooden spoon or handheld whisk until pale and fluffy. Add the egg and mix well. Add the vanilla extract, flour and baking powder and mix well to form a dough.

Roll into a ball, then wrap in clingfilm/plastic wrap and refrigerate for at least 1 hour.

Preheat the oven to 180°C (350°F) Gas 4.

Take the dough out of the refrigerator and remove the clingfilm/plastic wrap. Roll the dough out on a well floured surface, with a rolling pin, until about 35 x 40 cm/14 x 16 inches.

Spread the jam evenly over the dough, leaving a 2-cm/1-inch border around the edge. Roll the dough up from a long side. Cut into roughly 1-cm/½-inch rolls. Arrange the rolls, cut-side down, on the prepared baking sheets, leaving plenty of space between them, as they will spread when they bake.

Bake in the preheated oven for 12–15 minutes, until just golden.

Let cool a little before transferring to a wire rack to cool completely. Dust with icing/confectioners' sugar just before serving.

Cinnamon 'S' cookies

This is another grandmother's favourite, like the Spoon Cookies on page 126. We recommend that you bake a lot in one go because they store well in an airtight container for up to ten days.

200 g/13 tablespoons unsalted butter, softened at room temperature

170 g/generous ¾ cup (caster) sugar

2 eggs, lightly beaten

260 g/2 cups plain/all-purpose flour

2 teaspoons baking powder

3 teaspoons ground cinnamon

2–3 baking sheets, lined with baking parchment

Makes about 36

Put the butter and sugar in a mixing bowl and cream it with a wooden spoon or handheld whisk until pale and fluffy. Add the eggs one at a time, whisking well after each addition.

In a separate bowl, mix the flour, baking powder and cinnamon together and tip into the butter mixture. Mix well to form a dough. Roll into a ball, then wrap in clingfilm/plastic wrap and refrigerate for at least 30 minutes, or until firm enough to handle.

Preheat the oven to 180°C (350°F) Gas 4.

Divide the dough into six, wrap in clingfilm/plastic wrap and refrigerate for another 10 minutes.

Take each portion out of the refrigerator one at a time – you need to handle the dough cold, straight from the fridge. Roll the dough on a lightly floured surface into a finger-thin rope about 60 cm/24 inches long. Cut into 10-cm/4-inch lengths and place on a prepared baking sheet, curling them into 'S' shapes as you put them on the sheet. Leave plenty of space between them, as they will spread when they bake. Repeat with the remaining portions of dough.

Bake in the preheated oven for about 5–8 minutes, until just starting to turn golden.

Let cool a little before transferring to a wire rack to cool completely. Store in an airtight container for up to 10 days.

Gingerbread people

The mixture of spices makes these crisp cookies an all-time Christmas favourite, but they are delicious any time of year with tea or coffee. This recipe makes about 26 cookies, depending on the size of the cookie cutter and how much of the irresistible dough you eat even before the cookies go into the oven!

125 g/1 stick unsalted butter, softened at room temperature

125 g/⅔ cup (caster) sugar

100 ml/scant ½ cup golden syrup or honey/light corn syrup

1 egg, lightly beaten

260 g/2 cups plain/all-purpose flour

2 teaspoons bicarbonate of/baking soda

2 teaspoons ground allspice

2 teaspoons ground ginger

1 teaspoon cardamom seeds, crushed with a pestle and mortar

ready-made glacé icing, to decorate

cookie cutters in shapes of your choice

2–3 baking sheets, lined with baking parchment

Makes about 26

Put the butter and sugar in a mixing bowl and cream it with a wooden spoon or handheld whisk until pale and fluffy. Whisk in the golden syrup/corn syrup and egg.

In a separate bowl, mix the flour, bicarbonate of/baking soda and spices together and fold gently into the butter mixture to form a dough. Do not over-mix, otherwise the cookies will not be crisp when they are baked. Roll into a ball, then wrap in clingfilm/plastic wrap and refrigerate for at least 1 hour, or overnight if possible.

When you are ready to bake the gingerbread, preheat the oven to 180°C (350°F) Gas 4.

Take the dough out of the refrigerator and remove the clingfilm/plastic wrap. Roll the dough out on a lightly floured surface, with a rolling pin, until about 4 mm/¼ inch thick. Use the cookie cutters of your choice to stamp out shapes from the dough. Arrange on the prepared baking sheets, leaving plenty of space between them, as they will spread when they bake. Gather up the offcuts of dough and roll out and cut out more shapes. If the dough becomes too soft to handle, refrigerate for 10 minutes.

Bake in the preheated oven for 8–10 minutes, until nicely brown.

Let cool a little before transferring to a wire rack to cool completely. Decorate the gingerbread people with glacé icing. Store in an airtight container for up to 10 days.

Gingerbread cookies with dates

The finely chopped dates give a toffee-like flavour and texture to these cookies. Dates are also a good combination with all the lovely sweet spices. Simply dust with icing/confectioners' sugar to serve.

80 g/⅔ cup chopped pitted dates

2 teaspoons ground cinnamon

1 teaspoon ground ginger

1 teaspoon ground allspice

1 teaspoon bicarbonate of/ baking soda

300 g/2½ cups plain/ all-purpose flour

200 g/13 tablespoons unsalted butter, softened at room temperature

150 g/¾ cup light muscovado/ packed light brown sugar

2 tablespoons (runny) honey or golden syrup

1 egg, lightly beaten

icing/confectioners' sugar, for dusting

a small, star-shaped cookie cutter

2–3 baking sheets, lined with baking parchment

Makes 20–24

Put the dates, spices, bicarbonate of/baking soda and flour in a bowl and mix.

In a separate bowl, beat the butter, muscovado sugar and honey together with a wooden spoon until fluffy and pale toffee coloured. Add the egg and beat well. Add the date mixture and mix well to form a smooth dough. Roll into a ball, then wrap in clingfilm/plastic wrap and refrigerate for at least 1 hour, or overnight if possible.

When you are ready to bake the gingerbread, preheat the oven to 200°C (400°F) Gas 6.

Take the dough out of the refrigerator and remove the clingfilm/plastic wrap. Roll the dough out on a lightly floured surface, with a rolling pin, until about 4 mm/¼ inch thick. Use the cookie cutter to stamp out stars from the dough. Arrange on the prepared baking sheets, leaving a little space between them, as they may spread when they bake. Gather up the offcuts of dough and roll out and cut out more shapes.

Bake in the preheated oven for 8–10 minutes, until nicely brown.

Let cool a little before transferring to a wire rack to cool completely. Dust with icing/confectioners' sugar just before serving.

Frosted German-style gingerbread

These spiced cookies are the Finnish take on the German Lebkuchen. A retro 1970s favourite, we like its simple form and the contrast between the spiciness and the thick icing.

100 g/6½ tablespoons unsalted butter

150 g/⅔ cup honey

100 g/½ cup dark muscovado/packed dark brown sugar

100 ml/scant ½ cup milk

300 g/2½ cups plain/all-purpose flour

100 g/1 cup ground almonds

2 teaspoons ground cinnamon

1 teaspoon ground allspice

2 teaspoons ground ginger

½ teaspoon ground black pepper

1 teaspoon ground nutmeg

1 teaspoon bicarbonate of/baking soda

1 teaspoon baking powder

grated zest of 1 unwaxed lemon

2 eggs, lightly beaten

Icing

200 g/1⅔ cups icing/confectioners' sugar

½ teaspoon vanilla extract

2–3 baking sheets, lined with baking parchment

Makes 30–36

Put the butter, honey and sugar in a small saucepan and melt over low heat. Continue to cook, stirring with a wooden spoon, until bubbling and the sugar has melted. Remove from the heat and stir in the milk. Let cool a little.

Put the flour, ground almonds, spices, bicarbonate of/baking soda, baking powder and lemon zest in a large mixing bowl and mix well.

Pour the melted butter mixture into the mixing bowl. Add the eggs and mix with a wooden spoon until everything is well combined and has formed a sticky dough. Roll into a ball, then wrap in clingfilm/plastic wrap and refrigerate for at least 1 hour.

Preheat the oven to 180°C (350°F) Gas 4.

Take the dough out of the refrigerator and remove the clingfilm/plastic wrap. With floured hands, pull off about a tablespoonful of dough and roll into a ball. Place on a prepared baking sheet and flatten slightly. Repeat with the remaining dough.

Bake in the preheated oven for 12–15 minutes, until nicely brown.

Let cool a little before transferring to a wire rack to cool completely.

To make the icing, sift the icing/confectioners' sugar into a bowl and stir in the vanilla extract and 3 tablespoons of water. Stir until smooth and thick. Spread a teaspoonful on top of each cookie.

Store in an airtight container for up to 10 days.

Almond and raspberry tartlets à la Runeberg

The recipe here is a modern take on the original Runeberg tarts, which according to legend were the favourite of the 19th-century Finnish poet of the same name. The original recipe is made with breadcrumbs and rum. We've replaced them with polenta and fresh raspberries to give it a moist and crunchy texture.

125 g/1 stick unsalted butter, melted

2 tablespoons single/light cream

150 g/⅔ cup (caster) sugar

2 eggs

1 teaspoon baking powder

50 g/⅓ cup polenta/cornmeal

50 g/6 tablespoons plain/all-purpose flour

150 g/1½ cups ground almonds

1 teaspoon almond extract

75 g/¾ cup raspberries

Icing

40 g/3 tablespoons icing/confectioners' sugar

2 teaspoons hot water

a 12-hole muffin pan, greased and dusted with flour

Makes 12

Preheat the oven to 180°C (350°F) Gas 4.

Put the melted butter and cream in a small bowl and stir to mix.

Whisk the sugar and eggs in a mixing bowl with a handheld electric whisk until light and fluffy, then add the melted butter mixture.

In a separate bowl, mix the baking powder, polenta/cornmeal and flour together. Fold into the sugar mixture, along with the ground almonds and almond extract, until well combined.

Spoon a little of the mixture into the muffin pan holes, just to cover the base, then add 3 raspberries and top with the rest of the mixture so that the muffin pan holes are three-quarters full. Set the remaining raspberries aside to decorate.

Bake in the preheated oven for 15–20 minutes, until golden and risen. Let cool for 10 minutes before removing the tartlets from the pan, then let cool completely.

To make the icing, sift the icing/confectioners' sugar into a bowl and stir in the water until smooth. Spoon on top of the tartlets and decorate with the remaining raspberries.

Filter coffee		2.10
Latte		2.30
Short latte		2.00
Cappuccino		2.10
Mocha		2.60
Espresso		1.50
Extra shot		0.30
Tea		1.60
Hot chocolate		2.30
Water	bottle	1.20
Orange juice	bottle	2.20
Organic cordial	glass	1.00
Organic juices	bottle	2.20
Blueberry juice	bottle	5.90

index

credits and acknowledgments

I would like to thank the following people:

My friend and business partner Jali Wahlsten, who welcomed me to be part of Nordic Bakery's success; Jali's wife Marianna, who originally came up with the idea for the book and who has taken fantastic photos of our stores, and who has been a great support and source of ideas for creating all the recipes; my husband Mark Mink for his support and love; my parents Tuula and Matti Hulkkonen who introduced me to cooking and baking at an early age and managed to bring me up to appreciate the principles of baking breads yourself and using the best of ingredients; my friends who have been at hand to eat all the tested recipes and give feedback and comments; my nanny Jonna Savola who took care of my boys during the process of baking and writing;

my aunt Mirjami Männistö for lending her recipes; everybody at Ryland Peters & Small, in particular Alison Starling for believing in this book and being so excited about it, Céline Hughes for endless editing rounds and bringing it all together, Lauren Wright for PR, and Steve Painter and Leslie Harrington for great work on the visual side; book photographer Peter Cassidy and food stylist Lizzie Harris for beautifully presented food shots; Jane Milton and her team for testing recipes; Suomen Martat for inspiration on some recipes; all Nordic Bakery team members, especially Sini, Sanna, Andra, Vilma, Carl, Viktorija for their effort and creating such a lovely atmosphere in our cafés; Sami Wahlsten for going through some old school book notes for recipe inspiration; Jaakko Tuomivaara for Nordic Bakery graphic design.

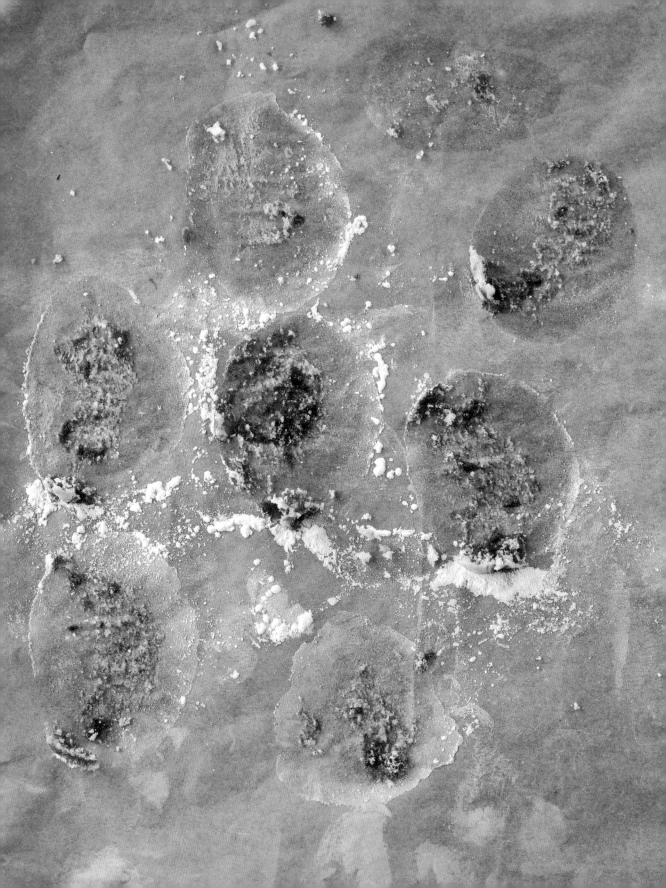